Acknowledgements

There are many renowned African-American authors who have helped pour the foundation echoing the truth. Even though documented proof harbingers the actuality theories, a deceit eclipse has covered the global world in a psychological shroud. The color of history was changed. Scientific law has become no more than mere observations, but truth rises to the top like the cream in milk. History no longer supports His-Story.

Cheikh Anta Diop, Dr. John Henrik Clarke, Ivan Van Sertima, JA Rogers, Lerone Bennett, Jr., Dr. Frances Cress Welsing, and Yosef ben-Jochannan are sojourners for truth. There are newcomers on the block including Runoko Rashidi and Ekowa A. Kenyatta. The authors provide clear rhetorical prose permitting the reader to hang from the knowledge tree of antiquity with the "Negro Cro-Magnon Theory" and exit out with the "Realization of Truth Theory" after realizing history books are nothing more than "European Mythology."

White Whores and Black Whoremongers is one of the most dramatic books in the annals of Black/White Race relationships and told from a unique point-of-view. The book portrays reasons for the rivalry and disenchantment between Black men and woman, and the varying philosophies for planned subconscious Black inferiority mindset turning Black/Edenic people into ghetto fabulous fools.

OPENING

The title, *White Whores and Black Whoremongers* (written in 1995 with a second printing in 1999, and again in 2007 and 2013), is sometimes misleading to a reader who thinks the book is about White prostitutes and Black pimps. The book realistically explicates the whoring of people with African ancestry. Four hundred years ago the whoring and devaluation of Black mankind started with slavery in the US. Today the whoring continues with the psychological leftovers minus the physical chains. Those who win the wars write the history books.

As a woman with African ancestry, I have watched Black men rushing to marry White women as a way to boost their emotional/social chances for Euroequalization. Twenty years ago these men say straight up, "It has nothing to do with color." "That is who I fell in love with, and she happens to be White." Currently, I hear just the opposite. "I only date White women." "Yeah," they say, "Black women are too aggressive, fat, angry, and mouthy." This outright comment leads to subliminal thoughts. Black men acquire psychological whiteness through their partners. Those who marry outside of their ethnic group do not bring with them cultural or racial pride to the altar. They are grasping for a psychological mainstream White status. When children are born, the White mother labels the children "bi-racial" to distance the offspring from African heritage. By giving the children a label helps reduce the blow to their very own individual psychics. It is self-forgiveness for having contact with a Black man. When you are something you aren't, it validates within your mind the misleading notion to jump on the bandwagon of conjured up erroneous racial classifications. With this action Black men actually foster the slavery on those people left behind. Remember, in his mind he feels he has escaped and will work to keep those he left behind shackled. He has become one of the Master's overseers.

Europe changed the color of history. The European documentation used to rewrite history exposes the real intention—a paradigm shift for genetic survival. European history has been powerful enough to destabilize nations in the world and promote European hegemony. All one has to do is look at the global maps. The only countries and nations in constant conflict and war are Black and Brown in skin color. With the sacking of ancient libraries in Egypt, Mesopotamia, Asia and the Americas and the rise of Nuevo-philosophical Hellenistic thought, the dominance of western philosophies has decimated the original African truth and replaced it with European myths (Ekowa).

A colonial and/or European education annihilates peoples' belief in names, languages, environment, heritage of struggle, unity, capacities and ultimately **in themselves**. It makes them see their past as one wasteland of non-achievement, and it makes them want to distance themselves from that wasteland. It makes them want to identify with that which is furthest removed from themselves - Ngugi Wa Thiong'o, (Kenya, *Decolonizing the Mind*).

We know mankind migrated out of Africa 80,000 years ago, but the Bible dates the Garden of Eden at about 6,000 years. The Bible says Cain went to the Land of Nod and knew his wife. Nod was east of Eden (REALLY). Introduction of the word "race" into the English language around 1580 implied inequality. At the time there were no systematic notions of racial differences in the global world. In 1684, Francois Bernier came up with distinctions of mankind based on physical appearance. In 1762, Carolos Linnaeus, considered the father of Modern Taxonomy, developed scientific and biological classifications to group species according to shared physical characteristics. In 1879, Social Darwinism placed Caucasians at the top of the species. Race was a means for the European conquest and colonization of Africa and slavery in the West. Colonialism unleashed the White man's reign.

The Euro-American scientific world gave Europe the licensing power to "naturally" dominate non-European indigenous populations. The advent of anthropology allowed individuals with certain physical and mental traits to succeed more frequently than others. Linnaeus' classifications became consistent with the Darwinian principal of Common Descent was revised. Today DNA sequences have blown the lies wide open.

Darwin's Theory of Evolution distinguishes the differences between races of man based on genetic branching and natural selection. His theory says that genetic branching is the process occurring when ethnic groups separate from one another, each developing their own genetic characteristics different from other groups. Popular at the time was the idea the Nordic Race of Northern Europe was superior evolvement in a cold climate.

It forced Nordics to develop skills. The skills evolving from their characteristics deemed them expansionists who were adventurous. Natural selection worked at a faster pace in the frigid north, eliminating the weak and unintelligent more thoroughly than it did in warm climates like Africa. Nordicists reasoned that if animals adapted to their own climates, both physically and mentally, then humans did as well. The leading anthropologists and psychologists of the day wholly supported those ideas. because of their

advanced survival

Preface

WHITE WOMEN ON PROWL

There are countless numbers of predatory White whores in heat and Black Whoremongers chasing their tails. Needless to say, Black women are losing ground as they compete with the monsters the White man has created. White women, placed high atop a pedestal—no matter how sloppy fat, snaggle-toothed, or butt ugly they are, the Black man looks through glasses prescribed in error by a Psychological Optometrist. It has caused rivalry and disenchantment between Black men and women.

As the Aryan Nation and KKK speak on talk and reality shows and hide behind sheets at rallies and parades loudly proclaiming a great "racial revolt," it is evident that they are wasting time. If you take a look around, you will see that there is a "silent racial revolt" going on minus the guns and hand-to-hand combat.

This "silent racial revolt," fought against the grain of White fathers and White families, who are trying to keep their daughters from taking off their thongs and panties. This action will leave an Aryan Nation in this country the size of Chicago in a few generations. Right now legislators are trying to get the racial category "multiracial" on the US Census. Millions of Black citizens in this country will become part of a "pseudo White Race," that is a tactic to reverse White annihilation when the multiple check off system is used to classify people in the US Census.

White women snare the cream of the Black crop. Black women who must divide the leftovers with drugs, violence/prison populations and alternative lifestyles share the balance. What is so ironic about the whole situation is that White women regardless of their economic or social status have the first pick. This includes White women with little or no education—career street walkers and topless dancers in clubs, i.e. the throwa-ways. Putting it another way, this type of woman does not represent the image the average man would take home to meet mamma.

The Black man does not consider the same standards when seeking a White mate. Just the fact that she is White overshadows all other attributes. When a Black man chooses a Black woman, she **must** be educated, good looking and have a good job. She can help him monetarily.

A Black man will accept a White woman under any circumstances. If she does not have the looks—so what! She has the White skin. If she does not have an education--so what! She can apply for a GED. If she has no money--so what! He will use his money to make her life more comfortable. If he is a man of financial means, once they are married, he might even use his money to set up her entire family and make them business moguls and financially independent.

No matter how many degrees or how white in color the Black woman is or how involved with the church, there is no way to compete. The Black woman may have the looks, the education, and the job, but she does not have the racial classification White. The Black man needs the racial classification of White to raise his selfesteem that started the "bottoming out process" in the 1600's.

We are in the midst of a racial holocaust folks, and nobody can stop the attraction of the White woman to the Black man. Reasons exist for what is taking place, but to stop its progress is impossible.

America lives in TV talk land, reality shows, video vacuums, and movie moralities. The visual is more believable than the written word because a large number of Americans do **NOT** read and in many instances can't read. The non-reader has started to appear on the college campus. America's colleges offer remedial classes to accommodate its ill-prepared students.

It is evident that non-readers have affected the way we live in this country.

Newspaper circulation has declined, and television cable stations have expanded. In fact, young people today center their lives in the middle of Internet social sites, television, music videos, and movies.

Young adults watch television 21 hours per week. As a result of our media mode lifestyle, broadcast elite's (ABC, CBS, FOX, NBC, PBS, and including cable networks) set the stage to convey constructed messages. Language is our basic tool to convey thought and speech, and mass media has the ability to control our lives with television images and word communications. Result: See the show, and the **entire** race is the **same.**

If the preceding premise is true, the media mode lifestyle in which people live make it easy to draw certain conclusions. The OJ Simpson, Clearance Thomas, Mike Tyson, Tiger "Negrito" Woods, Kobe Bryant, and Michael Jackson (before his untimely death) news stories surfacing over the years give enough evidence to prove there are no hasty generalizations presented.

Coverage of the Mike Tyson alleged rape case did not receive the same amount of coverage as the other stories which lead to the belief the missing ingredient was a White woman. Broadcast elites want the viewer to consider all links between plausibility and reasonability. Newscasters use plausibility, which persuade viewers to believe the message they want to convey.
The players in life (Republican Congress

Controllers, i.e. Dixiecrats, Evangelicals, and Wilsonians) have declared all Jokers wild Action, welfare and education. Labor Statistics released figures showing Whites held 88.8% of the managerial and professional positions in the work force. The figure was down 2.8% from the previous 10 years. In the same period Blacks held 7.1%, which had increased, from 5.6% or 1.5% in the same time period. Nobody needs the Bureau of Labor Statistics to prove a point. Go to corporate America and take a look around. It is just philosophically sickening to White man validate everything.

Even with the minimal increase in managerial and professional positions held by Blacks, there are references to the "angry White male" when answering questions about Affirmative Action. With the states moving to eliminate the claim of "reverse discrimination" in the workplace,

In their efforts to win the card game of life, the Dixiecrats (a White supremacist splinter-party of the Democratic Party) have become the masters of the game. They use media coverage to stack the deck in their favor. The broadcast media, in turn, gives daily assurance that conservative governmental policies add up to the magic *Blackjack* number of **21.**

Media coverage flexes its muscles when it wants to convey certain media messages. Television newscasters went to great lengths to present the Jackson, Thomas, Tyson, Bryant and Simpson stories, but the OJ Simpson Case stands out as the icon to promote certain beliefs, principles, and theories. The networks worked hard to present evidence, to project views, and to taunt and educate the White women in this country who prefer Black men.
relating to Affirmative In 2004 the Bureau of

After the arrest of OJ Simpson, the taunting seemed to surface. There was a global warning sent to all White women. "If you mess with a Black man, look at what will happen to you."

Since the first printing of *White Whores & Black Whoremongers, Beheaded for Execution*, and the coauthoring of *OJ Simpson's Double Jeopardy*, I found myself wanting to say much more about the aggressive nature with which White women are going after Black men. When the OJ Simpson preliminary hearings started in 1994 after the murder of Nicole Simpson, I became infuriated to find out that a man of his financial means, education, and looks had married an uneducated waitress who was also a drug user.

On the National footing White America had convicted OJ of murder after the day-to-day televised trial that pre-empted **EVERYTHING A-L-L D-A-Y every day!** He, in turn, has convicted himself for the murder of Nicole by showing frequent insane gestures. She helped him become part of the White Man's constructed society. He was able to move in and about the White World. She helped elevate his psyche, and the perceptually elevated this drug addict to the level of—Angelic—OH DEAR GOD!

After Nicole's death, America rose to the occasion and uplifted she and her "trailer trash family" to the status of "Princess Diana and the Royal Family" while turning OJ into an ignorant, shuffling buffoon. He still stimulates a momentum when the cameras flicker. He stabs newscasters with bananas on national television. He still hasn't learned his lesson and has been banned from his "make believe Caucasian" American Fairyland. You can't allegedly (I said allegedly) murder a White woman and get away with it—even a drug addict former waitress. It was obvious he still hadn't learned his lesson. He thought he could make money by writing the book, If, I had Did It. OJ, look at what has happened with your White woman exploits. You will never get out of jail. We ban you from mankind.

He offends and taunts White America. "How dare you marry a White woman, says they." How dare you kill a White woman," says they----OH! But-but-but she was my **Albino Queen says he!** I have the popularity, fame, and money to do what I want. I am OJ—the Juice! I am the greatest Running Back of all times.

It was about that time I started noticing formats on the television talk show circuit back in 1995. Montel Williams, for example, married a White topless dancer. He elevated her to one of the producers of his show and glorified daily to his TV audience—DIVINE WHITE WOMAN ENTITY!!! He told the TV audience—My m-o-th-e-r is half White--So I **is** equal to you—OH DIVINEALMIGHTY WHITE MAN!!!

Those Black men you see strolling along with White women at the local shopping malls are in actuality **pimp-smacking** their Grandmothers, Mothers, and Sisters to the ground for the offspring of ancestors who cut off **nuts and bolts.**

The women they grope have nothing to offer but the White skin on their bodies. Black men feel the need to receive a psychological "White man equalization feeling." The psychological White women preference by Black men is a created inner-self, egotistical boost Caucasians have self-created in their bodies and souls.

The scheme of things is logically clear. Selfesteem bottoms-out with the reduction of a person to the level of chattel and counted as three-fifths of a White person by the US Government. We dub you Black folks as second-class citizens. To become a first-class citizen psychologically, the Black man must possess all of the things Mr. Supremacy possesses including the White woman. (Your mind is playing tricks on you—you little trick.)

A White woman psychologically equalizes the Black man and makes him think he is atop the **ideal pedestal**. It is a two-way street. White women see Black men as more handsome, aggressive, exciting, and more sexually adorned than White men.

The media has also helped the Black man/White woman match-ups. Television in America uses verbal language, visual images, and sound to generate impressions and ideas to viewers. Viewers interpret what they see on television as reality. Media has the power to modify thought patterns and influence a person's day-today living.

The tightly constructed social stratification's put in place by Mr. Supremacy are becoming highly differentiated. To put it mildly, rip the seams apart. Will White culture controls pull the reins to stop the stampeding destiny of race and class?

America gets is daily dose of the Nation's once toprated daytime talk show Jerry Springer's "Swing Into Action Fight Fest." The shows producers because of protests by the American public have stopped the pugilism, chair throwing, and all other violence. On the show White women flaunt themselves before an American audience foaming at the mouth and showing their love for Black men who have enticed them with a slice of *the chocolate spice of life.*

America watches as Montel's format once included daily promotions of interracial couple ceremonies with Black man White woman **cavalcades** across the television stage. Black women in the audience have bigwide gapping smiles and clap harmoniously just like sheep drug from the pastures to the barn for shearing. Now Montel has the perfect crease in his mid section from bowing so much.

Over the next century, Caucasian anthropologists predict the concept of race will disappear. Caucasians amount to only 8% of the global population. Only 2% of White women globally are at childbearing age or younger, whereas, 6.3% of women in Nigeria alone are at childbearing age or younger (United Nations Population Information Bureau, 2010). Extinction (absorption) of the

Caucasian Race is a looming reality.

A Michigan State Law passed in 1995 created a Multiracial Category for all state education and other government forms. A Federal decision allows multiple check marks rather than a Multiracial Category Box for the 2000 Census.

Mixed race advocates are upset with the multiplecheck off approach as still in control" Caucasian America proclaims—*Once a Nigger—Always a Nigger*!!---The Mixed-Race Advocates declare loud and clear: You must sever our Black roots from their foundations--**We is White!"**-They just can't accept America's resolution that proclaims: Any person with African-heritage will be classified as Black!"

Example: After winning the PGA Black-faced Golfer Tiger (Negrito) Woods announced to America that he was "Cablanasian" and not Black. He confessed to the world that he did not want to be enshrined as the newest **BLACK** sports superstar. To add comedic flair to the story, his big-Black-faced father—looking just like he had stepped off a Mississippi Plantation—followed suit when he shed his Blackness to America and declared that he is not really Black! Tiger's mother is from Thailand where the indigenous population is Negrito. Tiger, you're more Negrito than you think.

The Woods family, like a large majority of Black Americans, helps White America reclassify African Heritage in the U S of A. It is a natural reaction for Blacks to emendate with *the sense of race* because it is a daily "wake-up" call.

America's aim has always been to alienate Black consciousness by creating a spoken and written hypothesis of "An Antiquity by the Caucasian Race." Seventy-three to ninety percent (75-90%) of all Black Americans are of mixed heritage. So the term "bi-racial" you hear people use doesn't mean anything. It is nothing more than a new mode of brainwashing. Do any of us fit into a neat slot? Multiracial advocates feel racial labels have personally affected them. White man equalization is at hand. The average American does not realize the lack of a psychological equalization. Unless there is an induced Caucasian connection, there will never be equalization. Creation of all humans started from one African mother, where is the "Mixed" Race in

America coming from? Confusion would be a better choice of words.

The perspective approach to history has been one of constructed mystification. Anthropology is a conjured up science for categorizing people and is blatantly wedged in erroneous idiotic sequences for mass stupefaction. The following statement is an example: Description of the indigenous Negritos of Australia--A "SPECIAL MODIFICATION OF THE NEGROID TYPE" by early explorers. Isn't that a statement of stupidity—a special modification? Why were they a special modification, and who modified them —GOD? The White man has always had a freaked out imagination that he discovered the world. Once he arrived in Asia, Oceania, and other termed "exotic places," he found Blacks already there. He couldn't explain his findings so he termed the "denials— refusals to explain" or "mysteries." As you will see, Africans were not contained only in the Continent of Africa.

Chapter 1 White GlobalAnnihilation

Two ancient skulls, one from central Africa and the other from the Black Sea Republic of Georgia, have shaken the human family tree to its roots, sending scientists scrambling to see if their favorite theories are among the fallen fruit. This skull is the earliest known record of the human family discovered in Chad (Central Africa). The new find was nicknamed 'Toumai' and comes from the little-known interval of human lineage.

Christopher Columbus knew that the African Mali Tribe had come to America almost 200 years before he set foot on American soil. Tiger Woods told America that he did not want to carry the label "African-American." He wasn't Black. People should keep their mouths closed if they don't know from whence they speak. What Tiger Woods does not mention is that his mother is an admixture of the Negrito from Thailand. The indigenous people from Thailand were Negroes in antiquity.

Blacks are the Original/Aboriginal Race of mankind and the admixture for all Brown and Yellow Races of mankind. The Negroid Race represents the color foundation for all colors. Look to the "color wheel" developed by a great White scientist. The world listens to a Caucasian constructed history that tells us Blacks made no contribution to human history. Ancient history has

recorded Adam and
although the ***Bible***

Eve were European-like people does not mention Europe in its contents. It is
hard for Euro-Americans to use common sense. Just read your Euro-centered
ancient history books. The history books say Rome invaded Egypt about 30
BC. If the Bible dates to 6000 BC, there were no White people running
around in the Book of Genesis or Exodus or Leviticus. Think about it. How
many times does the ***Bible*** mention Egypt and Ethiopia? OH!!! At this
particular instant the Author just forgot. European and U. S. physical
anthropologists have classified Ethiopians and all other North Africans as
Caucasian. Authentication of a European origin now exists.

Just look at what is happening. In 2001 Oxford University initiated a genetic
cluster study and then stated: *62% of the Ethiopians fall in the first cluster,
which encompasses the majority of the Jews, Norwegians and Armenians,
indicating that placement of these individuals in a 'Black' cluster would be
an inaccurate reflection of the genetic structure. Only 24% of Ethiopians
appear in the cluster with the Bantu.* In addition, some anthropologists have
argued Ethiopians' craniofacial features resemble those of the Caucasoid
Race. Scientists believe that modern humans originated in Africa, and that all
non-Africans carry a later mutation that occurs in Ethiopia today

Caucasians have stolen Negroid legacies from the beginning of time. Greek
Philosophy—Socrates, Plato, Aristotle and even Englishman Shakespeare
have been deemed as majestic and imperial Philosophers although we know
the philosophies come from the mouth of Aesop (560 BC). Socrates spent his
last days putting Aesop's fables into verse. Mohammed in the Koran used
Aesop as an authority (Rogers, J A, World's Great Men of Color, New York:
Simon and Schuster, 1996, 73). Caucasians have stolen the Black origin of
civilization.

Caucasians are dying out and need fertility drugs to carry on their lifelines.
Look at the increased births of sextuplets and other multiple births all due to
fertility drugs. The impromptu cloning of "Dolly the Sheep" became a
profound-mystical scientific discovery for the whole world to see. Suspect
tells the author that cloning of White people is close at hand.

The Caucasian Race has many albino traits. Caucasians lack melanin; and therefore, are pink in color. Albinos are jerky and uncoordinated in movement. Albinos lack the agility and strength to run fast and jump high. Ask yourself why people with Negroid heritage dominate professional recessive and disappear black, brown, and yellow genes.

The push is on to reclassify many AfricanAmericans as White—just as many Negroid people globally undergo a reclassification to Caucasian. Pay close attention to the Puerto Ricans, Cubans, Panamanians and other Latin Americans who come to the US and say that they aren't Black/Negroid. The USA has reciprocated and classified them as Hispanic. In the US, Hispanics are classified as Caucasian. Since there were three-quarters (3/4) more slaves taken to South and Central America, than to North America are the South Americans and island nations still White Latinos? The average person thinks Cuba and the Dominican Republic are Caucasian island/nations. Cuba is over 80% Black, but the Dominican Republic is a nation with a "mulatto" population.

Caucasian constructed history tells us that **Columbus discovered America**. American chronicles do not tell that Abubakari II had a Malian Fleet visiting the Americas in AD 1311 and 1312. Abubakari was a leader of Mali who sent 100 large fishing boats across the Atlantic Ocean in 1311.

Columbus himself made notes in his diary that he found dark-skinned people he assumed to be traders from Guinea, West Africa, trading with the native Caribbean people (Asante, Molefi Kete. African American History: A Journey of Liberation, Maywood, NJ: The Peoples sports. Caucasian genes are

once crossed with dominant Publishing Group, Inc., 1995). African sculptures have been located in the Mexican towns of Tres Zapotes, La Venta, and San Lorenzo. There are eleven colossal African heads sculpted in stone with heavy lips, full checks, broad nostrils, and braided hair. The African sculptures, each standing 9 feet and weighing about 40 tons cited in the works of several modern scientists (Asante, 22-23).

The Slave-owning US "Founding Fathers" legitimized slavery. White skin color and/or European origin became an immediate exemption from racial oppression. Today the barbaric actions would be termed a "paranoid schizophrenic feat of madness." The demented schizophrenic suffers from false perceptual experiences and hallucinations. The intense prejudice against Blacks globally is prevalent and quite common. "Negrophobia" –a term used to define the fear of Black people.

European and American historians have helped to falsify history. A constructed legend exists proclaiming that the superior White Race has always reduced Blacks to slavery. This enables Whites to justify the presence of Negroes in Egypt, Mesopotamia, and Arabia by decreeing that Blacks were enslaved.

Burned, buried, and bumped explicates Black Antiquity. The slave-owning "Founding Fathers" built a nation using the backbones of our ancestors while they legitimized slavery and excluded indigenous people in this here USA. We as people live in a world of day-to-day existence that does not matter because of Black folk dehumanization. A White woman must be at the end of a Black man's arm to make him feel a sense of Caucasian validated self-worth. Currently, White women are snaring Black men at alarming rates. To top it off the "Mixed Race Advocates"—the present "House Niggers" want to be re-classified and catalogued as White to elevate the good mental health of the Euro-American human psyche. Americans fall into the category of most blinded Americans who say, **"Don't tell me anything about race because it is a construct."** Maybe that is why everybody was so upset to see the people of New Orleans floating in the flood waters after Hurricane Katrina trying to "keep afloat" for three days before Washington got there.

Slavery in the Name of Jesus—White superiority was born within Christianity. The Roman Church of 1455 authorized infidel (atheist) people to servitude in 1457. The Council of Cardinals met in Holland and sanctioned as a righteous and progressive idea, the enslavement of Black Africans for the purpose of their conversion to Christianity and for acquisition in the labor market as chattel property. final outcome helplessness. Some slaves longed to be a replication of the "chosen ones"—the Master White Race. They loved their masters and allowed to bask in the "reflected White Glory," which in turn enhanced both Black and White psychological delusional power (Glory to His Name)!

Euro-American anthropologists are reclassifying, racially cleansing and then recapturing prototype Negroid people and categorizing them as Caucasian through artificial means. Imagined is artificial. are inconvenient counter-examples to Europe's central doctrines. Don't be brainwashed. The Black and Aboriginal plights are whore-a-causts.

The definition of a holocaust depends on who's won the battle, writing the history books and making the movies. The original Biblical Jews were of African Edenic Ancestry. Africans are the indigenous native Hebrews. Therefore, when God said: "Ye were a curse among the heathen, O house of Judah, and house of Israel; so will I save you, and ye shall be a blessing: fear not" (Zechariah

Slaves were incapable to foresee the and ingested the inborn learned

People of color America and 8:13). He was talking about "Black Abraham and Black Moses" and their descendents.

Some readers of my web site have blatantly told me that I have no right to take on the entire global world and should stick to African-American and Sub-Saharan African History. What the readers were trying to say was: "We have the history, science, anthropology books, racial classifications, and maps already written the way we want. Don't mess up or undermine our ideologies." I want to thank those readers for "turning on another light." The global world represents the whole puzzle. People of African descent are indigenous mankind of the global world. When you came to colonize, we were there.

Black History has been fragmented and destroyed like our families and lives. Scattered pieces of the trite and obscure rebuild what we have become and maps out where we are today. The old cliché states that history repeats itself and simultaneously recreates the wheel. God did not destroy his creation which has resurfaced to the top after buried in a makeshift grave for a few centuries. GOD, BLESS AMERICA!

The new Millennium brought with it a new world order. The global world is no longer homogenously White as you believe. There was a "changing of the guards" while America was busy painting its inhabitants White. While Blacks were proving to White America that they were—at least—part White. A series of events at the end of the Millennium spelled out White global annihilation.

Chapter 2 The Whore-A-caust

The Author's intentions are not to categorize groups of people but to correct false historical records embedded into our society. Slaves were solely one culture including solely one people with no differentiating characteristics— once a slave always a slave. Examples of physical features and dress/fashion emphasize certain points and give readers a needed W A K E -U P C A L L!

Whites in this country are sick of AfricanAmericans consumed by racial issues. Black peoples' lives center on the race issue; whereas, Whites feel that the topic of slavery in this day and age is irrelevant because slavery happened over 400 years ago. Whites feel discrimination no longer exists because of the passage of the Civil Rights Law of 1964.

Whites see slavery as a part of history while Blacks live a vivid day-to-day racial and cultural awareness or consciousness. God may have created life, but in this country slavery has shaped the path of all our lives.

Thousands of Black people have crossed the color line to pass for White rather than be part of the stigma of classified as the dogma of bondage and part of a "big categorical grouping." It is quite evident in this country that Black blood has infiltrated American bodies. According to one author 45% of presumed White Americans have some amount of Black blood (Mooney Race & Ethnicity, Chapter 3, 1998). Racial characteristics in the US are undergoing a state of absorption and quite likely reclassification.

Just sit on a bench in your local shopping mall and look at all of the **once** distinctive Negroid characteristics that some "**supposedly White** people" are born with-curly hair, protruding teeth with wide gaps between the two incisors or front teeth, and large round buttocks, large flat noses, and a sort of permanent suntan. Whites love curly hair, but would deny that curls are a cross between woolly Negroid hair and straight Caucasian hair. The curls are a distinct feature of Negroid blood. There are now hair care products available to "supposedly white people" to straighten frizzy hair.

Some Blacks are tired of the race issue because they don't want to admit categorization into one big cluster of people. A proportion of Blacks feel that if they can change themselves by assimilating into whatever the mainstream wants they can some how evolve into just being an individual.

When it all comes down to the nitty gritty, Black people are Black first and people second no matter what skin shade envelops their bodies. Blacks refer to themselves as black, medium brown, light, yellow, highyellow, light brown, bright, and brown in skin color, but Whites don't see Blacks in varying degrees of skin shades. To White people, Blacks are just "Black."

One day I tried again and again to describe who the teacher in Room 222 was to a White colleague. I referred to the teacher as "light-brown skinned" with light eyes. She looked at me as if I were speaking in a foreign tongue. When I made her realize who he was, she still didn't get it. She said strangely, "Light brown." "He's not light brown, he's Black." This was a wake-up call for me.

White people don't see Black people in different or varying hues and colors. Blacks are the only ones who see themselves as having different shades of skin or hair textures and eye colors because Black folk separated by skin color at the hands of the Master during slavery (Caste System). Blacks like to make the color differentiation within their own race, but Whites only see a Black person as Black with no color differentiation. Blacks like to make comments and profess that they are "part White" or "part Indian." Being part White makes people with African ancestry a little less Black and closer to White.

Newsweek Magazine published an issue that said to write articles about race for an interracial audience is a source of pain and vexation. It tests a person's loyalty to his own race while thwarting wholly all religious beliefs. Whites suspect that Blacks see prejudice where none exists. Whites feel that Blacks blame their own shortcomings while using the guise of Racism. Whites are tired of hearing about Black problems (Case, 57).

When the format centers around race on television interviews and talk shows, Whites always comment, "Why do you talk about Black and White so much?" "Why is race always an issue to you?" "Why do you say I'm prejudice?" I have Black friends and neighbors." "Why are you so angry?" "Quit blaming me because you can't get a job—You is just IGNONT." When it comes to discussing race, Americans might as well be watching different channels. Whites tend to deny that racial discrimination exists because they see the world "according to media portrayal snapshots."

Due to locality and/or residence some Whites have no contact with the Black Race in this country. Therefore, the race issue may not be an integral part of a person's day-to-day living, and there is nothing to base like or dislike opinions of a person/people in the Black Race unless he has read the latest issue of a news magazine or has watched the national news that evening. Sometimes it means reading between the lines or watching TV with great digression.

The only contact the White person may have is the contact through written words and television. Even the no-contact White person feels a sense of fear about Blacks because the media has instilled fear. There has been a derived "Negrophobia" attitude instilled in the American culture.

The written and spoken word in books, periodicals, and television have suppressed and dismissed the positive African-American historical aspects. Black historical accounts have been squashed and replaced with media blitz which show Black faces spread on photo pages and television screens when the topics forefront are drugs, crime, AIDS, and welfare.

The modern journalists show a callous disregard for ethics and responsibility. Mass media has become part of ethics and responsibility. Mass media has become part of 7). Media has conjured up a cheap life melodrama and twists facts to produce and increase profits. You can see it readily when thinking Simpson, and Michael Every form of media carried the stories.

A long history of mistreatment has caused the race issue obsession with Blacks. NBC's *First Edition* news program highlighted the growing problem of Black undercover policemen shot by other cops of their own squad. The show's commentator stated that because White policemen are suffering from race-based assumptions, they feel that all Blacks are criminals. Therefore, an undercover policeman who is dressed like any other person on the street without a uniform has to be a criminal because he is Black.

People of color in this country are readily stereotyped and linked to crimes. In the mid 1990's after the bombing of the Federal Building in Oklahoma City, Oklahoma, early reports told of two Middle Eastern men fleeing the scene. Since the bombing of World Trade Center in New York City, people from the Middle East have been linked firstly and facetiously to terrorism. about the Mike Tyson, OJ

Jackson news events of 1994. When Whites commit heinous crimes, reporters go to great lengths to determine what deep psychological reasons would have caused them to act this way. When Blacks commit crimes, sentencing and incarceration take place in lickety-split time.

Ordinary American citizens think that Black people and crime are synonymous. Both Blacks and Whites have become the victims of psychic homicides altering the National brain chemistry. Joe Feagin, author of *White Racism: The Basics* relate the dynamics of Whites blaming Blacks for crime because it is rooted in slavery and European images of Africans as violent savages. African men who rebelled against slavery became examples to feed hysteria and fear.

Painstaking measures by European and Western historians to hide and suppress Black historical accounts proving the origin history. Scientists mummies, prehistoric sculptures, hieroglyphics and drawings, tombs, and art relics that prove a **falsification** of history.

Blacks are the original/aboriginal race of mankind, the admixture for all brown and yellow races of mankind, were in the Americas before Christopher Columbus, present during the colonial period, fought in the Revolutionary War and the Civil Wars, built the telephone and telegraph system, settled the West but have been overlooked and dismissed in the history books as not having contributed anything in a positive way.

In Latin America alone there were 3,650,000 slaves, and by 1808 there were one million slaves in the United States (Ploski, Williams, 1-3) (Walvin, 63). In 1650 Blacks out-numbered Europeans in the Americas as a whole. How can oven baking six (6) million Jews ruminate the term "holocaust," and the

WHORE-OCAUST of 200 million Africans ignored?
of civilization hide in "revisionist"

have examined bone remains,

Slaves were packed and shipped in their own excrement to the Americas in cargo vessels. As Blacks embarked the journey here, their history, language, and culture flowed out with every bowel movement.

In 1492, there were 80 to 100 million American Indians in the New World. By the end of the Century there were only 10 million left. They could not survive the initial European conquest and the introduction of European diseases. Early Europeans disguise and
cupping, and
have been successful capping history since

translation of the Bible.

The word **whore** means prostitution means to devote or corrupt for unworthy purposes. The word whore, used as the title of this book denotes a **whore mentality** that has evolved as a conspiracy to destroy the entire Black race. This ***WHORE-A-CAUST* blasphemy** has taken place while promoting a "Christian path of righteousness."

The History : The Declaration of Independence, which contains the often repeated phrase. . . all men are created equal . . . was written by Thomas Jefferson, who owned about 200 slaves at the time and never set any of them free, including the his slave children fathered by Sally Hemings. Jefferson's words certainly had no reference to Negroes, who at that time had no place in American society except as property. White historians, who consider themselves experts of the Jeffersonian Era, were stunned after finding out Jefferson had slave children. In fact, it took sophisticated DNA Testing to prove Jefferson had fathered Black children for them to even fathom the thought. Get over it. Most slave masters had children by slave women.

The Constitution was written by and for "We the people and dedicated to ourselves and our posterity." All of the 55 delegates that met in Philadelphia to draft the were masters of

in masquerading, the King James

prostitute, and Constitution and all of the members of the 13 state conventions that ratified it were of the White Race.

The 14th Amendment is invalid for the following reasons: Failure of ratification by three-fourth of all the States in the Union according to Article 5 of the US Constitution. Out of 37 States, 16 rejected it. Many of the states counted ratified the amendment but were compelled to do so under duress of military occupation, and coercion automatically voided everything.

By unlawfully excluding 23 Senators from the US Senate, shows the failure of a Joint Resolution to adopt the Amendment by intent of the 14th original US Constitution and the Organic Law of the land. It did not, and could not; repeal anything that was part of the Organic Law. Therefore, the principles of precedent and stare diesis render it void.

Abraham Lincoln's Emancipation Proclamation of September 1862 said: I have urged the colonization of the Negroes, (back to Africa), and I shall continue. My Emancipation Proclamation links with this plan (of colonization). There is no room for two distinct races of White men in America, much less for two distinct races of Whites and Blacks. . . . I can think of no greater calamity than the assimilation of the Negro into our social and political life as our equal . . . Within twenty years we can peacefully colonize the Negro . . . under conditions in which he can rise to the full measure of manhood. This he can never do here. We can never attain the ideal Union our fathers dreamed, with millions of an alien, inferior race among us, whose assimilation is neither possible nor desirable.

Lincoln actually proposed an amendment to the Constitution that would not authorize Congress to recolonize all freed Blacks back to Africa. On August 15, 1862, Congress did appropriate over half a million dollars the Constitutional Congress. The Amendment is repugnant to the for that purpose. Thousands of Negroes had been shipped back when Lincoln was shot (Aryan Nation, *100 Facts: The Race War of Blacks Against Whites*).

Step one of the psychic assault started in the 1660's here in America with slavery. Slavery also started the fragmentation of the black family and the destruction of Black cultural and historical consciousness. Blacks had no reason to look at themselves as worthwhile individuals as part of the livestock on plantations. Registration of slaves by first name only, and after a few generations had no surname connections to past generations. Slavery represents the initial **brainwashing** of a whole race of people.

Family fragmentation resulted by selling family members from slave families; listing slaves on registrations and records as chattel along with other livestock; and not allowing the slave male/female to marry legally. The tactic of keeping the Black family from descending during slavery allowed Whites to rein supreme. Slaves were solely one culture including solely one people with no differentiating characteristics--once a slave always a slave.

This dissemination facade also started the disenchantment and rivalry between Black men and women. It was against the law for the Black male and female to be husband and wife, emotional separation evolved.

As a means of control, Slave Codes for certain unwarranted actions (Quarles, 27) kept slaves in line. Slave Codes did not recognize slave marriages. The masters assigned husbands to women who had reached the breeding age-- without any civil contract. Slaves conducted their own marriage ceremony —"jumping the broom" (Huggins, Kilson, & Fox, 123).

Virginia legalized slavery in 1661. After the American Revolution, slavery became firmly entrenched in the South (Logan & Cohen, 40). In Africa Blacks had been accustomed to strictly regulated family lives and rigidly enforced moral codes. In America slaves were dictatorially encouraged to adhere to the customs of their White masters and forget their language.

Caste and class systems communities created by the White masters. A Mulatto's (multiracial) social standing depended in a large part on the amount of White blood running through his veins. But entrenched in both White and Black minds was the following fore drawn conclusion. Horses and donkeys produce mules. Whites and Blacks produce mulattos. The masters created a hierarchy by giving each slave specialized tasks. The hierarchy used the method to control.

The separation Domestics and Artisans ensued. The artisans were carpenters, construction, and maintenance workers for the Ante-bellum mansions and considered the highest class of slaves. Domestics (house slaves) adopted the White pattern of respectability and were proud of their honesty and loyalty to the White family. Blacks who mastered the White man's language placed themselves automatically above other Blacks who had no mastery of the English language. Isn't the same true today?

The domestics, artisans, and foremen constituted the aristocracy of slave society; whereas, the low man on the caste system was the "field hand." House slaves were Mulattos who learned the master's manners and speech patterns. The house slaves often learned to read and write and took pride in direct contact with the Master, socially as well as intimately.

This intimate contact produced mulattos who in turn became part of the upper social strata in the "Big House." The mulattos had divisions: giraffe, tierceron, African customs and

existed in the slave quadroon, octoroons, etc. and were proud of their positions of responsibility, fine manners, correct speech, and clothing and flaunted their superiority over the "field slaves" (Huggins, Kilson, Fox, 120-3).

During the era of slavery, Blacks identified themselves with the White culture —forgetting theirs— the African culture. Black people suffered a psychological "confusion of identity" because the African culture reflected barbarism and savagery. The presumption was probably the same as it is today when foreigners come to the US. "If you are in America, you do as Americans do."

Plantation owners reinforced the creation of social strata classifications and directly contributed to creating self-worth based on the lightness of skin. Mulatto slaves in turn perceived themselves better because of the treatment. Once the mulatto slaves left the plantation, regardless of the lightness of skin, they were still "Negroes and Negresses."

The relationship between master and slave was nothing more than economic that is much like a modern day automobile assembly line worker and plant manager. The only place the Mulatto status was of any importance was within the Black Race. Once the Mulatto left the plantation, he was just another Black person. Blacks' past lives have created the "Value Whiteness" stigma that still **looms today**.

If the Mulatto slave was white enough in color to pass for White, he probably disappeared into the population creating some of the so called White people we see walking around with the nappy hair, broad noses, protruding teeth with wide gaps, round buttocks, and a sort of permanent suntan.

People profess, "We are all members of the human race! Color does not matter!" **WHY** have so many people **passed for White?** Whites were and still present themselves as wiser, more powerful, and more superior with the most ultimate authority in day-to-day situations.

Slavery caused major changes in this country after legalization in 1661. Black slaves became personal property of White men with no rights. During the 1600's there were White European indentured servants in the colonies. Indentured servants who no longer wanted to serve their bondage could escape into the frontier easily. They were not noticeable as run-a-ways because they blended in with other Whites.

Slave babies insured a continual supply of labor. Slave children fathered by both Black and White men inherited the status of their mothers, which made them slaves for life. Slave children fathered by **both Black and White** men inherited the status of their mothers.

Notice, there is no mention of White mothers fathering slave children because it was totally out of context. The White woman was on "sacred ground," and in an "untouchable" state. For that reason, the White woman positioned into a state of reverence and not violated **publicly**.

Because Africans were foreigners, outside of the protection of English Law, there were no official laws for protection. Slave Codes were enacted depriving slaves of human rights. The codes aimed directly at the slave marked him as socially inferior to Whites. In the Thirteen Colonies, the branded mark (black skin) was evident and outwardly seen by all. Any skin color darker than White skin became a badge or sign of slave status.

After 1700, the demand for Black slaves increased throughout the Thirteen Colonies. The slave population in the Colonies of South Carolina and Virginia grew more rapidly than did colonies in the North. The Southern Colonies were entirely dependent on slave labor; whereas, the New England Colonies had the least amount of slaves.

In the 1700's Willie Lynch, a slave owner, delivered a speech to other slave owners outlining three ways to keep salves in line. If the White man uses these tactics, the effects would last for hundreds of years. They were: 1) Pit men against women, 2) Pit old men against young men, and 3) Pit light slaves against dark slaves. Read further in this book. All three Willie Lynch standards are staunchly in place. His tactics are still at work today.

A so-called normal family life was impossible for most slaves. Slave masters did not hesitate to break up slave families when a profitable sale came along. Slave Code endorsement strengthened the slaveholders' power over the slaves. Slaves had to carry passes and show the passes to any White man who asked.

Reading, writing, and supplying books to slaves was strictly forbidden. Slaves could not raise certain crops nor could they buy or sell goods. All Whites were empowered to arrest run-a-way slaves. Black folks found themselves awarded as prizes in raffles, wagered in gambling, offered as security for loans, and transferred as gifts from one person to another.

"The Grace of God" that according justified slavery to the following arguments:

1. Slavery was necessary for the Colonies to achieve a high level of civilization.
2. Slavery would allow White men to create a great civilization in America.
3. Because Blacks are barbarians, the slaves made it possible for Whites to become part of a superior civilization.
4. White slave owners and politicians of the time claimed that both the Old and New Testaments of the Bible upheld human bondage (Logan & Cohen, 88-9).

CHAPTER 3 The Slave Masters

Currently, we have the same problem of "brain slavery" but created differently than 400 years ago when slavery was legal. We are probably on step 300,000 of the Black physic brainicide. Today the "overseer" for the slave master is the Welfare System and authors like Richard Herrnstein and Charles Murray who carry the title implanters. Herrnstein and Murray co-authored a book titled, The Bell Curve: Intelligence and Class Structure in American Life that showed up in bookstores in the mid 1990's.

Authors like Herrnstein and Murray have helped to implant ideas so the media elite's can bring the ideas to the forefront. We then have other writers who reinforce their ideas in national publications. Whites get a continual reinforcement of superiority, while Blacks get a continual reinforcement of inferiority.

Nathan Glazer, author of "The Limits of Social Policy," writing in the *New Republic* said that Herrnstein and Murray were motivated to write Bell Curve because they can justify what they have written. He said, "It is true. Black impoverishment in this country is directly linked to intelligence" (Boyd, 1F). Glazer is just helping his comrades and countrymen to promote long held theories. Generation after generation of theorizing a whole race of people has not stopped White women from rushing to taste the black fruit. Until there is acceptance that the human race is devoid of a White majority, the ideas will prevail.

Social programs have produced dependency but linking these programs directly to intelligence because a person collects welfare is just not logical. What seems more logical is the following scenario: A person can work at McDonalds for $8.00 an hour or sit at home and collect welfare $681 per month for a family just in food stamps. If you were in this situation, what would you do?

In the Mid-1990's FOX Television aired a new show titled *TV Nation*. The show's host reported that Cobb County, Georgia receives $4 billion a year in government entitlements, one of the highest in the US. Cobb County, Georgia is the home of our once resigned-surrenderedillustrious House Speaker Newt Gingrich.

While the residents of Cobb County showed their support for Ginglynch's

Welfare cuts, Welfare constituted only 1% of government subsidies to the County. Most of the government spending in the County goes toward retirement recreational facilities, a government made lake and its upkeep, libraries, and the Lockheed facility.

Georgia has 159 counties, but Ginglynch's **Cobb** County receives government handouts that amount to 13 % of what is spent **nationally** on AFDC. It's amazing that Newt makes sure where Federal Moines filter while he points a finger at the Welfare System. Teenage mothers consume $34 billion a year in welfare benefits. Unwed mothers average eight years on Aide to Dependent Children. *Newsweek* published an issue about families receiving government transfer payments.

The table on the table below shows that half of all families in this country receive government benefits—just not Black women on AFDC. The table also points out that the biggest percentage of government entitlements go to people who are on Social Security. The table does not show the 676,000 farmers who get $9.2 billion in subsidies. It confirms that dependence on entitlements-handouts run deep--not just for Black women on AFDC (Samuelson, 45).

Government % Entitlement Benefits Families Social Security 26 Medicare 24 Medicaid 12 Food Stamps 9 Unemployment Compensation 9 Subsidized School Lunch 8 Government Retirement 5 Aide to Families with Dependent Children 4 Supplemental Social Security Income 4 Energy Assistance 4 Educational Assistance 3 Public Housing 3 Veterans Benefits 2

ALL BENEFITS 52%

People who receive welfare benefits are not part of the social strata remembered from Sociology 101. The three social strata classifications, upper, middle, and lower divisions, and the term "underclass" emerged. This term must apply to people who are underemployed, under-educated, or appear to be under a rock. This underclass title equates a certain "tenement class' that has no regard for mainstream authority. The underclass breeds a culture of poverty, drug abuse, sloth, and savagery.

Holly Sklar, author of "The Upper-class and Mothers N the Hood," equates a stigma towards children who receive welfare benefits. The children carry labels from birth as pathological bastards of their mother's presence and their father's absence or "baby daddy."

Since slavery, Black women have been stereotyped and labeled as mammies. A mammy is an image given to a controlling Black woman who instilled the spirit of subordination to masculine authority. When a Black woman accepts welfare, reinforcement of the mammy syndrome reinforces itself.

During slavery, the women who took care of children while their mothers worked in the field carried the reference "Mammies." Slave women who took care of both Black slave children and the Master's White children carried the reference "Aunties." Black people call their mother's sister auntie, as opposed to Whites calling their mothers sister "aunt." There are a heck of a lot of images that have been carried over from slavery—aren't there?

Welfare recipients who collect AFDC carry the reference of welfare queens. The term describes a "breeder woman image" lazily collecting government checks and reproduces poverty by passing on her pathologies to her many children.

The Republicans in Washington proclaim they made history in the 1990's by reforming the Nation's costly welfare system. Individual states will now set their own guidelines for recipients.

Then President Bushlynch arrived on the scene and cut $1.1 billion from the food stamp program that helps the poorest people in the US buy groceries. The plan also included squeezing Medicaid, the scheme that provides healthcare for the poor, and cuts in drug subsidies aimed at veterans. Education programs facing the axe included some aimed at anti-drug efforts and literacy. The department for housing and urban development faced some of the biggest cuts. Mr. Bushlynch proposed a $3.7 billion reduction in spending, 11.5% of the agency's budget, with programs targeted including housing grants for the disabled, AIDS patients and urban renewal schemes. With all of the cuts in social programs the Pentagon received a 5% increase to $419.3 billion in the mid 2000's.

How does a person find a job if they are living in a community where there aren't businesses like manufacturing, and service industries like McDonalds? Most downtown or central city areas of our larger cities are no longer in tact because of the expansion of shopping centers in suburban communities.

Businesses within walking distance in large metropolitan areas like Detroit are corner grocery stores, gas stations, and video stores owned and run by Arabs. There are African-Centered beauty and barber supply stores, and nail salons run by Orientals. Fast food restaurants line almost every corner. These jobs pay minimum wages and serve as sole employment facilities for many people.

In the Detroit Metropolitan area there is not a mass transit system; therefore, people without cars are almost immobile. How does a person find a job with no transportation? How does a person find a job if they have no work experience or training? How does a person find a job in his own neighborhood when Arab owned businesses hire only their relatives? Foreign workers pay little or no income taxes. There are no secrets. Loopholes mean tax exemptions.

Arabs hire their own relatives and friends to work in the stores, gas stations, and video stores in the Detroit Metropolitan area. There are many tax credits based on citizenship. Non-Resident aliens participating in cultural or training programs in the United States are not taxed on compensation paid to them by a domestic corporation that have offices in this country. This exemption extends to compensation paid by a domestic partnership or a US citizen or resident under Section #5178 of the Federal Tax Guide Reports. Section #5180 of the Federal Tax Guide Reports, have tax reductions by treaty. If a tax treaty ratified by the United States and a foreign government, the treaty provisions, rather than the Internal Revenue Code governs the extent to which each government may tax residents of other countries.

The average automobile worker in Detroit has had to upgrade job skills to keep up with robots/robotics guided by automatic controls. How does a person collecting welfare stay abreast when the schools in poor communities can't afford books or paper, let alone adult education courses or computers?

During slavery children were encouraged to beg. Begging was good training to help Whites realize that their slaves were dependent on them for all forms of livelihood. Blacks lived the realization that they were dependent. The programmed cycle of dependency has the coded instructions (White

Encroachment Legislates Fix Authority Repercussion Environment). cycle. Long-term recipients are SUBSTANCE ABUSERS i.e. SYSTEM ABUSERS.

Welfare causes a psychological dependence, just like crack cocaine and liquor. Children need it to maintain a pseudo-comfortable physical and psychological state. Without welfare assistance, the user would be LITERALLY homeless. To kick the habit might be impossible because there are not a large number of "welfare re-hab centers." The Washington Administration and present Congress rearranged the welfare system, and made big cuts in the areas of adult education and training programs constituting the **welfare re-hab centers.**

The current welfare system encourages dependency with no other way out. The Welfare System acts like a spider web. If one escapes the web, then what happens? There is still in an unorganized mass of threads. The system bundles the recipient (prey) in silk (the measly $681 per month) before feeding on it. A person collecting welfare is caught in a sticky mass and is easily drawn up and eaten by the system. Black child parents are being encouraged by Mr. Welfare to have more babies; thus, increasing monthly allotments from Mr. State White Supremacy. The rivalry and disenchantment between

It is a vicious like long-term Black men and women caused emotional separation during slavery when slave marriages were against the law. Some couples performed their own marriage ceremonies "jumping the broom."

During slavery there was no regulated family life or enforced moral codes. Slave masters slept with slave women any time they wanted. Thomas Jefferson—one of our Founding Fathers is a prime example. It took DNA Testing for America to validate the fact that Jefferson had fathered Black children by one of his slaves. Slave families were unstable. These families were referred to as "mother and her children" without reference to a father or man. Definition of slave status and race streams mainline through the mother. That way no matter how many times a slave woman gave birth to children fathered by the slave master and no matter how White in appearance the child appeared, Black was the race definition. Slavery started the regression of the Black male.

Mr. Welfare—one of many modern day forms of slavery has created the same non-regulated family life. Black child parents are being encouraged to have more babies by Mr. Welfare to increase the monthly allotment checks. Again, these families can be referred to as "mother and her children" without reference to a father-man. Blacks rationalize or justify their own behavior by giving reasonable and/or rational but false reasons for certain actions. Black men proclaim in their minds, "I'm not like those other Black people the news media are always talking about." As a result of those feelings, he thinks there is some benefit psychologically to assimilate into the White culture. Assimilation begins with cultural absorption, and the easiest way to assimilate is with a White woman. With that in mind Blacks often make it known when communicating with others that they went to mostly White schools, lived in a mostly White neighborhood, or went to a mostly White college.

Blacks are the only race that refers to each other in a friendly/casual manner as "Nigger." Chinese don't refer to themselves as "Chinks." Arabs don't refer to themselves as "camel jockeys" or "sand Niggers." Whites don't refer to themselves as "honkies." This is the symptom of a **Selfhatred/destruction disorder**.

By uttering the statement, "I **cannot** identify with Blacks in the Ghetto," shows proof that some people are suffering from the learned behavior of the "fly in the milk" syndrome. As they are flapping at the lips, about "**cannot** identify," or "I am fortunate lifestyle," Mr. White Supremacy is **continuously lumping** him into the same **big group** category he puts every other Black person.

Because of the Value Whiteness Stigma created during slavery, the Black man feels a level of elevation if he has a light-skinned woman. If he has a White woman, the elevation takes him to the penthouse. The Black Race is color struck and sees beauty in light skin, light eyes, and straight or curly hair. Even those women who wear fake extensions throw the braids and ponytails from sideto-side giving themselves a fixation of having long flowing locks; which simultaneously produces a subliminal sensation of **Anti-Black**.

Black people have a fixation with light skin and curly hair. When a Black child has straight or curly hair, the parent purposely leaves the little boy's hair a little longer than normal so that an onlooker will notice the curly locks. Just look and you will see male toddlers with curly locks streaming down the shoulders. The curly hair serves as an elevation shot for the Black psyche.

In the 1950's and 1960's a White woman was almost out-of-reach for Black men. Twenty-six years ago mixed marriages were against the law (*Jet*, 32). The new millennium opened the "heavenly white gate." Now it is more prestigious to have a White woman--if available-than the light-skinned Black woman.

Chapter 4 America's Auschwitz

The familiarity is cunning and skillful. The US has its own Nuremberg hidden behind numerous provisos. The Nazis outlawed animal experimentation before World War II but allowed medical and chemical experiments on Jews and asocial persons. Currently, the United States has a Animal Welfare Act in place ensuring optimal care for the humane treatment of animals used in medical experiments but has done an about face authorizing and commissioning covert non-White human research. The "Great Holocaust" was relatively short compared to the current on-going global **Whorea-caust** by the US and European scientists.

Many similarities and connections exist with the atrocities of Auschwitz and the tragedies linked to slavery in the Americas. While Auschwitz has been termed the site of the Great Holocaust," with dedicated museums, books, and articles, "The Middle Passage," and the great racial autocracies in the Americas have been treated as two-line snippet in US history books.

• Nazi ideology/slavery included classifications of racial inferiority."
• Auschwitz/slavery was the center of a governmentsponsored system of slave labor.
• Auschwitz/slavery was the center of a huge system whose sole purpose was the destruction of an entire group of people based on racial inferiority.
• Auschwitz/slavery was a program of cultural genocide and murder.
Adolf Hitler ordered the extermination of Jews between the years of 1942-5. Before eradication the German Government used Jews to perform human

medical and chemical research in Dachau. The end of World War II had deliberately killed six (6) million Jews by the Nazis, mostly in Auschwitz. In every history book, Hitler's extermination of Jews carries the title: "The Great Holocaust." There are thousands and thousands of books and museum exhibits relevant to the topic with 7,000,000 research articles on the Internet about the "Great Holocaust."

The National Socialists or Nazi Party acquired sole political power at the national level in Germany in 1933. Like the US, Germany had a system of prisoner corrections facilities. The Nazi Party created a system of concentration camps in which slave labor was the norm. Auschwitz was the center of this slave labor system. It was the manifestation of a plan to exterminate people who spoke differently or with an accent, who looked differently, who acted differently, and who in the European context, considered a different race. Auschwitz was for all intents and purposes, the industrial production hub of a massive system of human extermination based on the fundamental principles of Nazi governance. The Nazi ideology created a hierarchy of racial inferiority. Extermination awaited those who arrived first at Auschwitz. Individuals who were deemed unfit to work" suffered death by phenol injections. Extermination awaited sub-humans--not killed according to Nazi ideology. There was a difference between the two concepts reinforced.

It was important for the German officers involved in genocide and maintenance of the slave labor system to understand their role. They were not mass murderers, but social engineers eradicating the harmful elements. This led to the creation of a Greater "Germania." The gassing method was the best and most cost effective method of extermination (Feinstein, Otto and Suprun, Mark. Auschwitz, Detroit: Wayne State University, 1998 pp+).

Hitler was in the know. He and other Nazis knew the real reason for wanting to exterminate Jews. Hitler knew that Jews weren't White and considered them less than human just as the US Government considered slaves as chattel and listed them by first name only as part of their animal stock. That's why it was acceptable in PreWorld War II for Nazis to perform medical and chemical experiments before eradication because the Jews weren't White. The question asked by Americans today is WHY the autocracies occurred in Pre-World War II Germany? Americans are saying: "Hitler was a madman." "Why would he exterminate the Jews?" Jews are not a race of people but a religion—SO Says the UnITED StaTes of AMerIca.

Do the Jewish people constitute a race of people? The majority of Jews in Israel/Palestine currently are not from the seed of Abraham. They are Khazar Jews (European). The origins of the Khazars are unclear. They are converts (Ashkenazi Jews). These Jews voted to bring in the Falasha Jews from Ethiopia to Palestine so they/Israel could lay claim to the "seed of Abraham." Historically, Jews have gone through stages of Black/White racial development—because the Jews in Israel now are Ashkenazi Jews. Stage one--conception-the state of Biblical Blackness, which has evolved into the final stage of full, blown adulthood Whiteness. In America the word "Jew" once meant "Race." After World War II, America flipped the switch and turned the Jews into a Caucasian Race.

The official and legal definition of Jews in Israel today has the following: Orthodox Jews believe that *only* the children of Jewesses are genuine Jews; the race of the father is irrelevant. The hematological research of Professor A. E. Mourant shows that all Jews throughout the world, with the exception of some small, semi-barbarous, and insignificant tribes of converts here and there, belong to the same race, having an admixture of at least 5 to 10% of Congoid (African/Negroid) Blood *The Genetics of Jews* (Oxford, Clarendon Press, 1978). Currently, articles pop up to get people to distinguish between the "Jewish Afro Hairstyle," and the "African American Hairstyles." Arabs and Jews are sometimes referred to as Solomonids." Solomon, the Son of David—King Solomon, one of the Great African/Edenic Hebrew kings, was from the family line of Shem and Ham. Solomon, the king of Israel throughout Israel's finest years of prosperity, was a son of King David, and the successor to his throne. His lineage can be scripturally traced as far back as Rehab the Black Canaanite," or harlot, who was a descendant of Ham's fourth-born Canaan (Josh. 2:1; 6:1; 17, 23, 25). Originally, all Hamites and Shemites (or Semites) were Black (Bible, 943-4).

Moses, the author of Exodus, the second book of the Bible, was the great African/Edenic leader and lawgiver through whom God brought the Hebrews out of Egypt, constituted them a nation for his service and brought the Jews within reach of the land promised to their forefathers. Moses belonged to the tribe of Levi, to the Clan of Kohath, and to the house or family of Amram (Ibid, 85). The ancient name of Egypt in Hebrew is Mizraim, who was a son of Ham (son of Noah).

Moses was a Hebrew descendent of Abraham, and the Egyptians were a Black African people. Also, Jethro was the Midianite shepherd priest whom

Moses studied with and whose daughter, Zipporah, he married. He was from the line of Ham and Shem. After the death of his first wife, Sarah, Abraham married the Hamite woman Keturah and fathered six sons. One of them named Midian, the father of the Midianites. Jethro's daughter, Zipporah, was an Ethiopian in the Bible (Num. 12:1). Thus, one could conclude that Zipporah's father is from the line of Ham (Ibid, 89). Moses was married to an African Midianite Priest's daughter.

The Jewish people, the first branch called Semitic, descendants of Isaac, were the products of crossbreeding-Negro origin. In the Bible (Genesis and Exodus) are simply the conditions with which the Jewish people were placed from the beginning (Ibid, 120-21). The similarities are much like the Puerto Ricans, Cubans, and other Latin Americans grouped as Caucasians.

Readers must remember that there were four times as many Black African slaves delivered to South America and Latin America than the US. The Black and Brown in color: Pakistanis, Grimaldi Spanish, Italians, Arabs, Dravidians, Aborigines, and Somoans are just a few of the groups carry the reclassification of Caucasian by Euro-anthropologists and geneticists within the last century.

The Canaanites (Black Edenic People) and White tribes, symbolized (represented and/or characterized) by Abraham and his descendants (Isaac's lineage) blended to become in time the Jewish people of today. The man found in Canaan in prehistoric times, the Natufian, was a Negroid. In the Bible when the first White Races reached Canaan, they found a Black Race. The Canaanites were descendants of Canaan, brother of Mesraim, the Egyptian, and Kush, the Ethiopian, sons of Ham. Two hundred million Africans brought to the Americas tightly packed in slave ships, died en route from scurvy, smallpox, starvation, and suicide. The 15 million who survived the voyages to the Americas were only a fraction taken from the African Continent. Slaves were packed and shipped in their own excrement in cargo vessels. As Blacks embarked the journey here, their history, language, and culture flowed out with every bowel movement. This should be termed the great Urine and Defecation WHORE-A-CAUST or just plain SHIT!!! In 1808 there were 3,650,000 slaves in Latin America alone compared to the one million slaves in the United States (Ploski, Williams, 1-3) (Walvin, 63). In 1650 Blacks out-numbered Europeans in the Americas as a whole. Killing six (6) million Jews is considered a holocaust, and the WHOREOCAUST of 200 million Africans an oversight? The word whore means prostitute, and prostitution means to devote or corrupt for unworthy purposes. Using the work whore denotes a "whore mentality" evolving as a conspiracy to destroy the entire Black Race.

In 1492 there were 80 to 100 million American Indians in the New World. By the end of the Century there were only 10 million left. The Aboriginal would not survive the initial European conquest and the introduction of European diseases. Why isn't this murder and extermination of the American Aboriginal referred to as a Holocaust?"

The Scientific Method used in research laboratories to ascertain a controlled result. The so-called "Scientific Method" uses a covert or subversive tactic for Black Race suicide and destruction. A power practice generates a preliminary layout so that the ideas come from within the target population itself. Inward turns the guns. The Scientific Method uses 5 steps to eliminate people of Negroid origin medically, chemically and psychologically. Here's How To Do It! The US and European Governments use non-Whites as guinea pigs for medical and chemical research. During the years of 1935 to 1942 the Nazis outlawed animal experimentation but allowed experiments on Jews and asocial persons. The Nazis' experiments lasted about 10 years; whereas, the EuroAmerican Auschwitz human research connection has been ongoing for hundreds of years. The International Military Tribunal established an American investigation and tried 22 top Nazis in Nuremberg, Germany after World War II. The trial lasted from November 1945 to October 1946. The US titled the experiments: "Nazi Rule viciousness." Pay attention to the following excerpt:

The Avalon Project: Nazi Conspiracy and Aggression (March 1943) Volume 3
TRANSLATION OF DOCUMENT 002-PS

The surgeon general SS (the elite Nazi Party police unit Schutzstaffel) and police have blueprints showing special experts for Research in pharmaceutical chemistry, dental and clinical services and a special section of scientific service with the establishment of the following institutes: 1) Central Institute for Medical Scientific Exploitation 2) Institute for the History of Medicine 3) Pharmaceutical Pharmacy for Institute and 6) Hygienic Research Institute.

"War Crimes Against Humanity" by Yale Law School tells of experiments conducted in Dachau in August of 1942. Nazi leaders Adolf Eichmann put in charge by Adolf Hitler killed 6,000,000 Jews and performed just a few of the following more popular medical experiments:
Chemistry Research Institute 4)

Military Requirements 5) Pathological

1. High altitude experiments in pressure chambers
2. Experiments to determine how long human beings can survive in freezing water
3. Poison bullets
4. Injection with Contagious diseases
5. Sterilization of men and women by x-rays and other methods
6. Injections of chemicals in babies' eyes to turn the color from brown to blue

Probably the most famous experimentation perpetrated on Black folks was the Tuskegee Syphilis Study (1932 - 1972), but more "people of color" globally than any other are probably experiencing losses of life with the current experimentation. The AIDS Virus invented and designed to eliminate Black and Brown people globally, equal the most devastating epidemics to be unleashed on humanity.

Boyd Ed Graves, JD discovered the US secret 1971 Special AIDS Virus Flow Chart in 1999. American (EURO) scientists who created AIDS believe the anthropology textbooks documenting indigenous groups of people who inhabit all parts of the global world are Caucasian. The scientists, therefore, felt safe to develop a disease that would wipe out all people with Negroid Ancestry. Little did the scientists know that only 8% of the global world is Caucasian/WHITE! Many of the indigenous people (now classified as White) are dying of AIDS because their skin Brown. In effect, Caucasians have become victims of their own propaganda!

US Secret Virus Program: Black people have a gene called CCR5 Delta 32+. (Brown people have it too.) On the opposite end of the spectrum is CCR5 Delta 32-. The CCR5 Delta 32- is a mutation of the original CCR5 Delta 32+. The only people who have the Delta 32- gene are White people--Nordic Europeans.

The 32- allele inherited from both parents ligates immunity from the test tube created HIV and AIDS. The mutation does not have the required receptacles needed to "hold on" the HIV and AIDS Disease. The gene gives credence to the disease as racially designed to eliminate "people of color."

"people of color."

mutation. The incidence is only 2% in central Asia, and the mutation is completely absent among East Asians, Africans, and American Indians. The HIV/AIDS enzyme is the product of many steps in the laboratory according to all scientific criteria in every independent 'de novo' review that has been conducted to date. The science history shows an Aryan obsession with development of ethnic biological weapons targeting people of Negroid descent. At present it is unclear exactly when the *genociders* learned there was an exploitable difference in the blood of the Negroid Race.

Shortly after the United States Congress appropriated money (for offensive biological weapons) to the CIA and US military in 1957, Negroid children on the Continent of Africa became afflicted with a "new" cancer (Burkitt's Lymphoma). In 2002 something or some new disease was killing African children that utilized the CCR5 delta 32 positive. It became clear there was a clear master plan to debilitate, incapacitate, eradicate and eliminate the Black populations of the world.

Role Of The Ccr5 Delta 32 Allele In Resistance To Hiv-1 Infection In West Africa: The National Library of Medicine determined the frequency of the mutant CCR5 delta 32 allele in high-risk HIVexonerative Africans compared with the general African population, and assessed its in vitro protective efficacy against HIV-1 infection. In the homozygous form, the CCR5 delta 32-allele confers resistance to macrophagetropic (M-tropic) strains of HIV-1. Assuming that genetic characteristics favoring HIV resistance would prevail in a high-risk HIV-seronegative population, they examined the CCR5 genotypes of female commercial sex workers (CSWs) from Dakar, Senegal, who have remained uninfected for an elongated period.

The Results Follow: They confirmed the presence of two CCR5wt/delta 32 genotypes among 139 individuals (1.44%). PBMCs from these 2 heterozygous individuals were less susceptible to in vitro infection by an M-tropic HIV-1 primary isolate. The following were conclusions: Evidence of an increased prevalence of the CCR5wt/delta 32 genotype in a high-risk HIV-seronegative cohort in West Africa. Furthermore, reduced susceptibility to HIV-1 infection among heterozygous individuals supports a role for 32-bp CCR5 deletion in HIV-1 resistance.

The Stormfront White Nationalist Community commented: In the mid 1990's, an exciting new example of intense selection against one of the homozygotes for a trait came to light. This stemmed from the discovery that some people do not get AIDS even if repeatedly exposed to the virus (HIV) that is responsible for this usually fatal disease. The people who are immune have inherited two copies of a rare mutant gene known as CCR5-delta 32. They are homozygous. Those who are heterozygous apparently have a partial immunity or at least a delay in the onset of AID's. Approximately 10% of Europeans now have the CCR5-delta 32 gene variant, but it is extremely rare or absent in other populations of the world. There is a surprising connection in this story.

The CCR5-delta 32 gene also provides immunity to a deadly disease of bacterial origin, bubonic plague. People who are homozygous for the OCR5-delta 32 gene variant are completely immune, while heterozygotes have partial immunity. It is very likely that this life-saving allele occurs as a random mutation and that it selected for by the devastating black plague epidemics that swept over Europe beginning in the 14th century. During the first wave of plague, between 1347 and 1350, one fourth to one third of all Europeans died from this disease. Natural selection favored those who by chance had inherited the CCR5-delta 32 gene variant. Repeated waves of plague over the next three centuries resulted in an increase in the frequency of CCR5-delta 32 in the European population.

The Proof for the Development of AIDS US Public Law 91-213 signed March 16, 1970, by Richard Nixon states: "In the United States' effort to 'stabilize the population of Sub-Saharan Africa' and thus, increase the national security of future United States, Nixon proclaims there would be 'explosive events' (relative to John D. Rockefeller's, III oversight on the problem of African overpopulation). If the United States is above board, then the President should take immediate corrective action to fully disclose this secret (Manhattan-style) program.

Caig Venter, Jr., holds the patent to the gene called the "African American HIV/AIDS Entryway." This is the same gene that early US science used on African children in the late 50's (CCR5 Delta 32 positive).

According to the scientific world in the 18th and 19th centuries, Africans did not experience pain nor any form of heat sickness. That made them ideal candidates for laborers of the field. idea of using these surgeries to "expand medical knowledge" which would lead to "unparalleled global medical breakthroughs."

The medical and chemical research activities used on "people of color" were much like the tactics of eradication used at Auschwitz. The urban areas are much like concentration camps where the atrocities occur. Dr. James Marion Sims, President of the American Medical Association in 1876, and was heralded for his experimentation on Black slave women. Because it was illegal to read and write—an offence punishable by death, the slaves left no account of their ordeals (Brinken).

Along with the scenario came the same people for experimental

Dr. James Marion Sims 1845 – 1849: In a makeshift hospital he built in his back yard, Dr. Sims experimented with gynecological operations on a countless number of enslaved African women without anesthesia. Many died because of infections. Because of his experiments, he received the illustrious title, "Father of Gynecology." Along with the women used in experimental surgeries, he also opened the skulls of young slave children. He moved their bones around to see what would happen with the misaligned braincides.

The Mississippi Appendectomy (1930-1960): Eugenic Sterilization Laws were responsible for the involuntary sterilization of more than 200,000 men, women, and children.

1931 Dr. Cornelius Rhoads, under the auspices of the Rockefeller Institute for Medical Investigations, infected human subjects with cancer cells. He later goes on to establish the U.S. Army Biological Warfare facilities in Maryland, Utah, and Panama, and named to the U.S. Atomic Energy

Commission. While there, he begins a series of radiation exposure experiments on American soldiers and civilian hospital patients.

1940 Four hundred prisoners in Chicago-intentionally infected with Malaria in order to study the effects of new and experimental drugs to combat the disease.

1942 Chemical Warfare Services begins mustard gas experiments on approximately 4,000 servicemen. The experiments continued until 1945 and made use of Seventh Day Adventists who chose to become human guinea pigs rather than serve on active duty.

1947 The CIA begins its study of LSD as a potential weapon for use by American intelligence. Human subjects (both civilian and military) subrogated without their knowledge.

1950 Norfolk Naval Supply Center Contamination: US military researchers of biochemical warfare in the 1950s conducted race-specific experimentation. In 1980, the US Army admitted that Norfolk Naval Supply Center contaminated with infectious bacteria in 1951 to test the Navy's vulnerability to biological warfare attack. The Army disclosed that one of the bacteria types chosen because Blacks were more susceptible to it than Whites.

1950-1970 INDOCHINA: During US military involvement in Laos and other parts of Indochina, Air America flew opium and heroin throughout the area. Many GI's in Vietnam became addicts. A laboratory built at CIA headquarters in northern Laos did nothing but refine heroin. After a decade of American military intervention, Southeast Asia had become the source of 70% of the world's illicit opium and the major supplier of raw materials for America's booming heroin market.

1955 Army Chemical Corps continues LSD research, studying its potential use as a chemical incapacitating agent. More than 1,000 Americans participate in the tests, which continued until 1958.

1956 US military releases mosquitoes infected with Yellow Fever over Savannah, GA and Avon Park, Fl. Following each test, Army agents posing as public health officials test victims for effects.

1957 The Army Assistant Chief-of-Staff for Intelligence (ACSI) authorizes field-testing of LSD in Europe and the Far East. Testing of the European population is code-named Project THIRD CHANCE; testing of the Asian population is code named Project DERBY HAT. 1965 Project CIA and Department of Defense begin Project MKSEARCH, a program to develop a capability to manipulate human behavior through the use of mind-altering drugs.

1958 Prisoners at the Holmesburg State Prison in

Philadelphia subjected to dioxin, the highly toxic chemical component of Agent Orange used in Viet Nam without their knowledge. The men studied for development of cancer, which indicates that Agent Orange had been a suspected carcinogen all along.

1959 CIA and Department of Defense implement Project MKNAOMI, successor to MKULTRA and designed to maintain, stockpile and test biological and chemical weapons.

1968 CIA experiments with the possibility of poisoning drinking water by injecting chemicals into the water supply of the FDA in Washington, DC.

Tuskegee Syphilis Study (1932 - 1972) : The United States Public Health Service sponsored the Tuskegee Syphilis Study. They American Eugenic Society sponsored the study. The group was a sophisticated White supremacist organization, (today known as the Society for the Study of Social Biology). The Society was composed largely of scientists from a number of disciplines, along with wealthy philanthropists who used their foundations to finance the study until they were able to get the full cooperation and support from the government. Many of the elected or appointed officials in high-level positions within the government cleared the way for full government sponsorship of the program.

1969 Dr. Robert MacMahan of the Department of Defense requests from congress $10 million to develop, within 5 to 10 years, a synthetic biological agent to which no natural immunity exists.

1970 Funding for the synthetic biological agent obtained under H.R. 15090.

The Special Operations Division at Fort Detrick, the army's top-secret biological weapons facility, carries out the project, under the supervision of the CIA.

1970 United States intensifies its development of "ethnic weapons" (Military Review, Nov., 1970), designed to selectively target and eliminate specific ethnic groups who are susceptible due to genetic differences and variations in DNA.

1975 The virus section of Fort Detrick's Center for Biological Warfare Research is renamed the Fredrick Cancer Research Facilities and placed under the supervision of the National Cancer Institute (NCI). It is here that the US Navy, purportedly to develop cancercausing viruses, initiates a special virus cancer program.

1970 GI Heroin Epidemic : The CIA denies being part of the epidemic, but there is evidence to support the charge the agency had something to do with the GI drug addictions. The strongest evidence comes from the Vietnam War era when the CIA turned a blind eye to South Vietnamese leaders, such as President Nguyen Van Thieu, who were up to their eyeballs in heroin trafficking that hooked thousands of American Black GIs.

Native American Sterilization 1972-1976: Federal funds funded the massive project. Basing the federal trust relationship with America Native tribes based on numerous treaty rights and agreements includes the availability of medical services and physicians for Natives. As stated in the American Indian Policy Review Commission's report on Indian health, the federal responsibility to provide health services to Indians has its roots in the unique moral, historical, and treaty obligations of the federal government. No court has ever ruled on the precise nature of that legal basis nor defined the specific legal rights for Indians created by those obligations.

1978 Experimental Hepatitis B vaccine trials, conducted by the CDC, begin in New York, Los Angeles and San Francisco. Ads for research subjects specifically ask for promiscuous homosexual men.

1986 According to the Proceedings of the National Academy of Sciences (83:4007-4011), HIV and VISNA are highly similar and share all structural elements, except for a small segment that is nearly identical to HTLV. This leads to speculation that HTLV and VISNA are linked to produce a new retrovirus to which no natural immunity exists.

1987 Department of Defense admits that, despite a treaty banning research and development of biological agents, it continues to operate research facilities at 127 facilities and universities around the nation.

1990 More than 1500 Hispanic babies in Los "experimental" measles vaccine that had never been licensed for use in the United States. CDC later admits parents were not told of the experimental vaccine injected into their children.

Edmonston-Zagred (E-Z) (1991) : In 1991 in Los Angeles, California the Los Angeles Times reported that a thousand Black and Latino infants, some as young as 6 months old, were injected with the unlicensed measles vaccine known as Edmonston-Zagreb (E-Z) and given to infants both high and low doses. The vaccine, administered to over 200 million children worldwide, linked to an increased death rate among infants in Senegal, Guinea Bissau and Haiti, according to the Centers for Disease Control and Prevention (CDC).

It was clear in the Senegalese study published in The Lancet in 1991 that the infants were closely monitored and given extraordinary access to medical care, yet were still dying at the rate of 1 of every 13.3 injected with E-Z high titer, nearly all before their second birthday. (Awadu, Keidi Obi. LACCARCE, 6 July, 1996).

1980's - 1990's HIV - AIDS: There are a number of scientific journals trying to prove that the HIV virus originated in the Green Simian Monkey whose home is the west part of Africa around Zaire and then spread to humans. Green monkeys carry the disease SIV-Simian Immunodeficiency Virus that is the counterpart to the six-month old black and Angeles are given an human HIV virus. Scientists cite many theories that have evolved as ancestors to the AIDS Virus. One of the most credible theories is the Tom Curtis Theory. Hundreds of thousands of Africans 30 years ago resulted in contamination with a monkey virus for an experimental polio vaccine made from monkey kidneys.

The vaccine administered by the Winstar Institute
-a Philadelphia research organization. The Hot Zone (Richard Preston-
Random House - 1994) helps to verify the Curtis Theory. He writes of
diseases more deadly than AIDS. He tells of a new disease called EBOLA--a
virus transmitted from monkeys to humans.

1990's Crack Wars: Colombia - An agency of the US government sold
drugs to its citizens. The *San Jose Mercury News* reported a series of articles
that questioned the CIA's involvement and agency's role in America's War
on Drugs." The Mercury News investigation claimed that the CIA supported
a drug pipeline from Colombia, South America the San Francisco area that
may have financed the Nicaraguan Contras by selling tons of cocaine to Los
Angeles street gangs. In effect, the US government, through one of its
agencies, may have financed the crack cocaine boom that began in the mid
1980s.

In 1989, the United States invaded Panama and kidnapped Gen. Manuel
Noriega, at the time America's number one bogeyman in the War on Drugs.
Noriega was tried and convicted in a US court and is now behind bars for
life. What was lost in the thrill of victory, however, was the fact the CIA had
tolerated the general's drugrelated activities for more than 15 years because
he was a good ally against communism.

1994 Senator John D. Rockefeller issues a report revealing that for at least 50
years the Department of Defense has used hundreds of thousands of military
personnel in human experiments and for intentional exposure to dangerous
substances. Materials included mustard and nerve gas, ionizing radiation,
psychochemicals, hallucinogens, and drugs used during the Gulf War.

1995 Dr. Garth Nicolson uncovered evidence the biological agents used
during the Gulf War, manufactured in Houston, TX and Boca Raton, FL and
tested on prisoners in the Texas Department of Corrections.

According to the Nuremberg Code, drawn up after World War II as a result
of Nazi atrocities, The Declaration of Helsinki, adopted in 1964 by the World
Medical Assembly and revised in 1975, states that medical research on
human subjects should be based on adequately performed laboratory and
animal experimentation. It is crucial to distinguish between animal rights and

animal welfare. Black people are still disposable. Traditionally non-whites have had no political voice and therefore will not be heard even when we speak it holds no credence.

The scientific community supports animal welfare, which means guaranteeing the health and well being of animals used for research. Conclusion: Non-Whites do not have the same protection as animals. The US government has passed laws for the humane treatment of laboratory animals for experimentation of drugs, but the same laws have not protected human beings for medical experimentation.

Chapter 5 White Race Suicide or Black Race Absorption (The 8%)

An Advocate for Truth : In the US citizens are part of an audience carefully and systematically led to a particular set of beliefs? US citizens are manipulated and maneuvered. The documentation made by the founding fathers and existing political leaders represent the general population who mandate specific social and political changes. Ancient Babylon fell because she made all nations drink of her fornication—Babylon the Great, the mother of Harlots and abominations (Rev. 14:15-17). Rome fell because of its greed. The Caucasian aborts its White babies. Caucasians use covert activities to eliminate "children of color." Atonement comes in the form of a barren/infertile nation that will cease to exist.

"The Bottom Line" generates physic attitudes planted secretively, minds coerced into regularity and routine until one believes what is being reported as the absolute truth—v*ia the media*. In turn, there are psychic awards" developed for citizens who repeat the desired behavior. And you probably think it only happens in Russia, Cuba, Iran and the movies.

Covert Activities happen in the Western World too. The Author documents Covert Activities used as Psychological Operations at home and abroad. As a result, America remains in a ***supreme state*** globally. Long-term programmed messages and cultural abuses are kept in front of the population in quantity and volume to warn citizens and confirm in people's minds the reality of programmed **public policies and opinions**."

The Definitive Program: Caucasians are fighting for the reversal of White Race Suicide." Currently, there is a fight wagering--The First Law of Nature: Self Preservation.

Impending Falsehood : US citizens believe that Caucasians are a majority worldwide. Recounted by the United Nations Population Bureau is a drastic Caucasian diminishment. A few Whites know about their impending demise. The following is a quote taken from the *Fourteenth Word Press,* a White Nationalist Group based in Idaho:

The White Race derived from the Nordic and Alpine sub races of Europe amount to 8% of the earth's population. Only 2% is White female of childbearing age or younger. The life of a race is in the wombs of its women. Yet under the existing media, religions and governments, the last White women induced to mates with non-Whites wholesale . . .

The controlled media deceives the White Race by calling the colored races minorities" when they are 92% of the Earth's population, thus, disguising their genocide campaign against Whites by implying that Whites are a secure majority.

The last hope for the preservation of the White Race is massive and immediate distribution of the truth, such as this flier exposes. Act now with the fanaticism of desperation.

There are 66 countries in Europe and represented 23% of the global population in 2000. Europe has growth rates of less than 1% per annum. At the current rate Europe's population will take more than 380 years to double. A level of 2.1 European births annually would be required to balance the European death rate.

Within three generations (less than 300 years) the following is bound to happen on a worldwide scale. Presently, Whites amount to 8% of the global population. Look at the current situation as a racial quota formula. In 300 years Caucasians will represent about 1/16 of the childbearing population.

Let's look at an empirical racial quota formula using 16 as the control number. Within 300 years the average person in America and Europe will have the following 16-grandparent breakdown. There will be:

1 White grandparent
4 Chinese
Asian--including India and 3 Southeast Asia and the Middle 3 Black African
2 Latin American (Black/Brown)
2 From the Caribbean Basin (Black/Brown) East (Black/Brown)

The outline is already unfolding on the North American Continent and in Europe. Since the Caucasian gene is recessive. GUESS WHAT? It will disappear altogether. The United States and Europe have experienced severe labor and military manpower shortages as a result of their declining and aging populations. Presently, low fertility rates have produced a high ratio of retirees (baby boomers) to workers increasing taxes and social security expenditures. Armed forces must compete for both money and people, but less overall money exists because the productive population base has shrunk.

Between the years of 2000-2015 the population of the US and other Western regions will increase by 120 million. The population of less developed regions will increase by 1,727 million. Forty-five percent (45%) Western Africa's population in under the age of 15 (**eyes open**, child bearing age) even with the threat AIDS (Cline, 1+) (United Nations Population Information, 1+).

A British study said that AIDS is spreading so rapidly in Africa that the worst areas will show a net population loss rather than a gain in a few decades. In Vietnam, the situation appears even worse since the first AIDS case was reported there in 1990 *(AIDS and the Prospects of Population Decline,* BAOBAB PRESS, Vol. 4, No. 14.

The deliberate use of dirty medical instruments to vaccinate Africans (Garrett, Laurie, Albuquerque Journal, 10E – Jan. 1994) and Western **Caucasian implanted AIDS**" has not worked to eradicate the Black Race (Welsing, Frances Dr. The Isis Papers, Chicago: Third World Press, 1991). Both acts can be termed "biological warfare." A boomerang and/or backlash has triggered White worldwide rout.

In Nigeria childbirth rates equal 6.3 per female. The rate is 4.5 times higher than the combined European nations of Russia, Denmark, Germany, Hungry and Austria--The Author said **combined**. Caucasian females worldwide have childbirth rates of less than two percent (2%) per female. In 1990 the average childbirth rate for women in Haiti was 7.0 per female (Population Reference Bureau, 1+).

Nigeria expects to double in size in 2009, and triple by 2024, and quadruple by 2035 adding 312 million people to the world's population in 50 years. By the year 2035 Nigeria expects to surpass both the United States and the Soviet Union to become the third largest country in the world. Within 30 years Kenya, Ethiopia, Zaire, Tanzania and South Africa will be among the world's 25 largest countries (*The Incredible Pentagon Report: What it says about AIDS and Population Control* BAOBAB Press, Vol. 4, No. 14).

Impending Falsehood : Census workers can't add but sure know how to subtract. Elementary is the process if you realize what's happening. Black Race counts numbered 18-22 million in the 1960 US Census. The 1990 US Census utilized the calculated; guess **method of estimation** to tally numbers.

Black Race counts estimated at 30-33 million. The Black birth rate is 1.3% **above** the national White birth rate of 1% per year (Peterson 1+) (Population Reference Bureau, 1+)-**Wake up call folks**!

But there was a 10% African-American under count in the 1990 Census. Black women from Puerto Rico, Panamanian, and Cuba all counted as Hispanics. We all know that in 1808 there wee 3,650,000 African slaves delivered to Latin America compared to 1,000,000 delivered to the US (Ploski, 1-3) (Walvin, 63). Results: In 2004, there was a 66% under count of Black Americans so the 30-33 million is incorrect. It should be 55-70 million.

There continues to be a day-to-day psyche implantation processing technique. The conditioning will psychologically bluff a nation of White mothers with Black children and some Blacks sucking on White sponges as the white polish oozes nationwide. The US is giving Blacks a choice to become Pseudo White/Multiracial. Either wake up or suck up--It's dripping from your lips.

More than half of all physical anthropologists believe that biological races no longer exist. The anthropologists profess they should not continue to fix racial identity. If physical anthropology were one's vocation and practice in life, why would the group of scientists denounce their occupational training? Physical anthropologists can no numerical arrangements.

Population Policy currently recite that **is important** to realize that skin pigmentation **no longer denotes** racial classification. Indigenous people are being absorbed into the larger gene pool at alarming rates state the anthropologists and geneticists who write:
longer justify methodical

Planning: Anthropologists

The genetic diversity of people now living harbors the evolution of our species. Genetic heritage is vanishing.

African-Americans are so busy calling each other the Caucasian created word "Nigger," there is no realization that White folks have a hidden agenda for Caucasian genetic diversity diversified in the racial circle of " **White Only**."

History, geography, and methods of research have hidden the words Canaanite, Egyptian, Berber, Cushitic—(Ethiopian), and Semitic under the racial classification **Caucasian.** Webster tells you that all of these titles belong to indigenous Caucasoid peoples of Northern Africa. Don't insult my intelligence is what you should be saying to yourselves. When was a Caucasoid ever indigenous to Northern Africa?

It is here that the Phoenicians (Negroid People) were once the naval power of the Mediterranean. The Phoenicians traveled and joined the civilizations of Mesopotamia, Egypt, and India. This is where the Arabic people got their black/brown skin. This is where people of India got their Black skin.

It is here that Hiram, who was King of Tyre from 970-936 BC, became a friend and associate of Solomon and built Solomon a fleet of ships. Hiram then joined in expeditions to the East Coast of Africa.

It is here that you find out that Berbers and Arabs mixed and exchanged languages. Research books say Berbers and Arabs have Caucasoid facial features; therefore, they are Caucasians. Negroid features appear among members of scheduled casts--those who were enslaved--not the indigenous people of the continent. The amount of melanin found in ancient Egyptian mummies contained in the epidermis would classify Egyptians as Negroid (Diop, 238).

Impending Falsehood: The Black Power Movement was no more than Black Rage. The FBI and CIA were able to discredit African-American leaders by using a Divide and Conquer Method. The intended aim was to break up the cohesiveness of the Black Race. After slavery Splinter Groups," African-Americans broke away from the ethnic main body. That is why there are Black Race loyalists and Black Race traitors who want to be Caucasian-like. Black Race cohesiveness is not a strong point on which to dwell.

You can ask and then turn around and answer yourself: "Now I know what happened to Malcolm X, Martin Luther King, Huey P. Newton, Idi Amin, Marion Berry, Ron Brown, OJ Simpson and Clearance Thomas." It logistically was set up to fall into place from an organized effort on the part of the American Government.

Since the psychological guns are inwardly turned, the ideas now come from within the target Black population itself. The White man can sit back and view the show as it terms Black Neighborhoods as "degenerate urban populations that are degraded morally and ideologically." Whites believe that they are on the brink of extinction when they write:

Oblivion need not come in the form of physical destruction. It may simply involve the loss of habitat. Whites once occupied Harlem, Watts, East St. Louis, and many other Black neighborhoods. The arrival of Blacks (or other non-Whites) in sufficient numbers makes it impossible for Whites to survive; whereas, the process does not work in reverse. Even without the carnage of interracial crime, elimination of Whites happened through sheer loss of territory. Viewed in biological terms, ethnic diversity is prelude to destruction.

The audience systematically follows a particular set of beliefs. Whites feel that Blacks are very accommodating to egalitarianism--meek and considerate to mankind and are accepting of multiculturalism. The belief: Whites fear Black people because of intimidation tactics aimed at Black neighborhoods, schools, and the Black population in general.

Let me tell you the old-old story used to undermine the beliefs and loyalties of a whole population. In the mid-1960's there was a movement termed "Black Pride." James Brown had a popular song titled: "I'm Black and I'm Proud." The hairstyle of the day was the Afro. Even the traveling incognito White Michael Jackson had an Afro hairstyle along with a big nose and brown skin. Blacks wore dashikis. Blacks chose African names for their newborn children.

The Black Panthers emerged as an organized group in 1966 and so did **Black Power**. All things worked together to repair psychic damage caused by organized segregation and discrimination. Positive self-images emerged. To prove self-equality Black men wanted White women at the end of their arms because being equal meant having the same thing the White man had. Having a White woman was *Black Power*. White women were esteem builders and prize possessions.

The media turned **Black Power** into **Black Rage**. As the 1960's progressed, *Black Power* groups turned into *opposition groups* to designate the **Black Underclass**." Images surfaced and Black males depicted as criminals. White fear and resentment emerged and so did the excuse to build bigger, better jails.

An FBI memorandum from 1968 provides evidence of what transpired invisibly at he highest levels of the US of what transpired invisibly at he highest levels of the US 601 (April 2, 1968) was the product of a "counterintelligence program" run by special Agent Raymond N. Byers of the San Francisco office. The subject was "racial intelligence.'" *(Propaganda in Theory and Practice: How Does It Work? (Johns Hopkins University Press, p. 38)*

The memo provided detailed evaluations of all "Black Nationalist" movements represented in northern California, their leaders and members. The memo recommended ways in which the government might diffuse, censor, and distribute **revolutionary** literature. Americans see Black organizations as **revolutionary** and capable of **overthrowing** the US Government.

The memo made appeals to print and video media and the FBI gave insurrections to distribute the contents through a medium that reaches the entire "Negro population." Papers and magazines use their methodology to make the Negro accept this material. The FBI entangles with US democracy in a peculiar situation. We believe that we live in a democratic country - everybody knows that, everybody says it, it's repeated, it's dinned into our ears a thousand times, you grow up, you pledge allegiance, you salute the flag, you hail democracy, you look at the totalitarian states, you read the history of tyrannies, and here is the beacon light of democracy. And, of course, there's some truth to that.

The United States is a very complex system. There are elements of democracy; there are things that you're grateful for, that you're not in front of the death squads in El Salvador. On the other hand, it's not quite a democracy. And one of the things that make it not quite a democracy is the existence of outfits like the FBI and the CIA. Democracy based on openness, and the existence of a secret policy, secret lists of dissident citizens, violates the spirit of democracy.

The FBI cable noted: "The Negro youth and moderate must be made to understand that if they succumb to revolutionary teaching they will be dead revolutionaries." It is better to be a sports hero, a well paid professional athlete or entertainer, a regularly paid white or blue collar worker....than a Negro who may have got even with the establishment....and gained for him and his people the hatred and distrust of the Whites for years to come.

People tend to approve of a statement made by someone who is in some way similar to them in skin color because of cultural abuse and cultural manipulation. That is why most Black men are criminals, all Black female teenagers are pregnant, collect welfare, and strung out on crack.

The image of Black males as criminals became a national obsession in 1988 when Daddy George Bush made a bid for the presidency. He used the issue of the parole of a Black man convicted of raping a White woman as symbolic of Black males in general. Willie Horton became an image that thrived in a racial climate of growing White fear and resentment (13). The symbolism of "Willie Horton" was an organized effort of subversion presented to the American public by a respected White authority figure running for president of the US. The American audience made the behavioral change because the Willie Horton expression went public.

Whites share customs and common values with other members of the groups to whom they belong. Because of the long-term psychological abuse which has taken place in the Black community, it is very easy for Blacks to absorb Caucasian Theories as gospel. In essence, a White person is more credible than a Black person. Whom do you believe?

Caucasian stronghold—the united front! How can so few Caucasians have a stronghold worldwide? Puzzlement will follow the thought process, but there is a very simplistic answer. It can be termed the diplomacy of **coalition**. It might be termed the exalted emergency of a worldwide **Caucasian coup d'etet**.

Since 1910, 1% of South Africa's inherent Caucasian Ruling Class has had dominion over 99% of South Africa's native majority. The White National Party that ruled under Apartheid used their authority to designate freedoms based on color. Today 8% of the total world population dictates 92% of all inhabitants.

On January 1, 1942, 26 nations led by the US, Britain, the Soviet Union and China signed a joint declaration subscribing to the Atlantic Charter that later developed into the United Nations. The countries pledged their full resources to concentrated military coordination, exclusive alliances, recognition and interest in all global affairs.

When organized nations come together, regardless of their size, the power of decision looms on the horizon. The US along with nations in Europe has become great power spheres on every side of the planet. Organized as world powers, they don't have to worry about total opposition and can lend assistance to oscillate the destinies of the entire globe. The US is in control of all financial institutions. It owns the **World Bank**.

Impending Falsehood : Culture and birthrate. Look! Take a look here! After having been pushed to the very edge of the Earth, the **Caucasian Driven Evolutionary Process** has surfaced, and it look-id like suicide for the Black Race. White power practices and strategies globally are leading to White

Race suicide.

Whites cater to children by giving them everything from clothing and toys to their own private bedrooms, automobiles and lots of quality time. The modern approach is time out when a child flies into a rage, goes into a tantrum, screams obscenities, and throws things. The result is a generation of youngsters who are selfcentered, insecure, and demanding because of lack of discipline. The result has been the school shootings that have occurred in the past year in Paducah, KY, Jonesboro, AR, and Springfield, OR.

An old tradition in science proclaims observation drives changes in scientific theory. White anthropologists have made the observation they are vanishing from the face of the Earth and must act with a quickness to presume a shift in scientific interpretations.

Nations with populations over 30 million pose the biggest threat to White annihilation. They are the Republic of China, India, Brazil, Nigeria, Pakistan, Egypt, Bangladesh, Indonesia, Japan, Mexico, Vietnam, The Philippines, Iran, Turkey, Thailand and Ethiopia.

Yet--there may be no danger of White annihilation. The natives of India, Brazil, Pakistan, Egypt, Bangladesh, Iran and Turkey have been either **classified or reclassified** as Caucasians (Boyd & Asimov, 55). Ancient history tells us that inhabitants from these countries were people of Black Ethiopian decent and/or (Negroid people) who migrated out of Africa to new locations.

Asians, Indians, Indonesians, Mexicans, Ethiopians, Japanese, Pakistanis and Ethiopians with ethnic values do not declare: "We IS White!" "We is all White!" Once these Black/Brown people get in the US, immigrants from Mexico, India, Brazil, Pakistan, Egypt, Bangladesh, Iran, Turkey, Puerto Rico, Arabia and Ethiopia have been classified as Caucasian once they have entered the boarders of the US.

In the US and Europe Black/Brown global population growth represents a threat to the status quo, to political dominance, and social stability. But the **White Warrior rank and file** has plans to hoodwink the general earthly population.

There is currently a man-made evolutionary process underway to reclassify the world's populations as Caucasoid. Scientists now claim that race classifications are merely languages of the laboratory. Johnn Friedrich Blumenback, the German Scientist who established racial classifications in 1795 (Gould, 65-7), would rise from his grave and walk. He is one of the scientists who classified Negroid people as ape like" and Caucasians as the most beautiful people" on Earth.

Briefing agendas placed before the American audience in the form of video and print media. At the start of a performance like a great American Classical Broadway Show, the Offensive Opposition Troops—FBI, CIA and military leaders group together in a huddle to decide what maneuvers to use. The US introduces a global power play **ESTABLISHING** itself as the world master.

The US has perfected a global military presence for decades. Its escapades in Korea, the Cuban Missile Crisis, Vietnam and the Middle East, in particular Iraq -- used as psychological arsenal all in the name of psychological warfare. In the 1970's, the US Government called Korea, Cuba, and Vietnam covertly sponsored activities (Rositzke, Harry. *The CIA's Secret Operations: Espionage, Counterespionage, and Covert Action*, Westview Press: Boulder, CO 1988)

Almost the same rules sanction the alignment of a Defensive American Approval Troops to be strategically side-by-side which makes them more flexible. The psychological formations of a global military presence face the opposing third-world team at the line of scrimmage. The main responsibility in the past was to defend against passing plays by deflecting the Ball of Communism away from the potential pass-receiver and declare AMERICAN VICTORY.

Korea, Cuba, Vietnam and the Middle East served as ideological battlegrounds. Originally, the **tiny** countries spelled with a **tiny** "t" were considered developing or non-aligned" with the rest of the world-"Third World" countries. The so-called Third World Countries" with the help of an offensive orchestrated warfare agenda became worldwide threats"--organized by the US government--NOW LISTEN!!! DO YOU GET THE POINT-- PSYCHOLOGICAL WARFARE!!!

The US created hostilities toward the government and its people flourished, as many-sided battlegrounds became threats to the so-called free world—all in the name of Anti-Communism. The media painted the illusion of a meaningful change taking place that eliminated the oppressive form of Communistic government and killing off as many Black/Brown people as possible.

The team took its position in Korea, Cuba, Vietnam, and the Middle East. It formed a balanced line to manipulate and plant attitudes with an American audience. Military Leaders (centers) headed by the FBI and CIA snapped the ball in their court. A routine maneuver on the part of an offensive approval team punted Anti-Communism as far up imagery battlefields as possible all Communism. The now established world power structure recovers fumbles and gains possession of the big-bad" Supremacy Ball.
the many-sided

in the name of

CHAPTER 6 Population Control: Jail/Welfare

Statistics show that child parents are the largest producers of this country's jail population. According to an article that appeared in *Time Magazine,* a single juvenile parent raised more than half of the juvenile offenders serving prison time. Sixteen-year-old predators are coming from mothers 12-16 years old at the time of birth (Gibbs, 24-33). One out of every three (33%) Black males between the ages of 20 - 29 in the US have offenses that put them in the court/prison system.

In some cases incarceration provides a **better** quality lifestyle than being on the "outside." Prisons provide inmates with three meals, television, an education, medical and dental care, and exercise rooms.

On the street and in some communities jail-life provides a **better** quality life than one gets by living in urban America. **Comparison:** It costs $50,000 annually to support **one** prisoner. Each school district in the State of Michigan receives $7,600 per child enrolled in its school system. It costs $5,052 annually to support a family of **three** on Welfare. These figures just don't **jibe**. Does one create the other? Has prison become a technique for population management and management of certain segments of society? Is it social engineering resulting from national security policies illustrative of an evolving Fascist ideology within American politics?

Prisons make up a lot of the Nation's Growth Industries. In a 10-year period of time, for example, 16 new prisons built along with several minimum-security camps in California alone. This represents an increase of 40,524 high-security prison cells.

California alone spent over $5 billion on planning; engineering and construction of new prisons and the resultant bond debt will double that figure when interest payments equate into the final expenditures in the mid 1990's. The estimated cost of adding new maximumsecurity prison cells exceeded $113,000 per unit in the state of California and $85,000 per unit in the federal prison system. California's rate of $60,000 per minimumsecurity cell was twice the national average.

In the same time period Texas spent $1.5 billion to add 80,000 cells. News reports revealed the completion of LA County's new 1800 bed Twin Towers Lockup cost $373 million - a whopping $205,000 per bed! The rise of the "prison-for-profit" industry has been significant since its reintroduction in 1984. An increasing number of corporations are competing for lucrative contracts to warehouse convicts.

Further fueling the Nation's investment in imprisonment, the sponsored Crime Control Act of 1994
committed $9.85 billion toward prisons, including $7.9
billion for state prison grants and $1.8 billion to reimburse states for the incarceration of undocumented immigrants.
America had already reached the second highest rate of incarceration in the industrialized world with 519
of every 100,000 persons in the US locked up in the mid 1990's. The Sentencing Project: This rate was 22 % higher than and 5 to 8 times higher than most industrialized nations. The US rate of imprisonment exceeded only by Russia (558) and followed by South Africa (368) under the White racist social policy of Apartheid. This stood in stark contrast to other nations' rates such as China with 111 per 100,000 and at the other extreme, Sweden with

minuscule 4 citizens jailed per 100,000 (*Covert Action Quarterly*, "Private Prisons: Profits of Crime" Fall, 1993, Amerikkka, *The Police State*). Since there are so many non-readers, the visual is the convincing factor. The audience rises and falls to your expectations. The statistical information on the next page confirms that as many Whites commit heinous crimes as Blacks (Adler, 22). An observer might think that Blacks commit ALL homicides after watching the national news. The visual is the convincing factor.
In the mid-1990's there were 24,500 homicides in this country. The chart below gives statistics of who kills whom?

White Victims White Offenders 5,967

White Victims Black Offenders 1,216

Black Victims White Offenders 392

Black Victims Black Offenders 6,600

Black males are over represented by nearly 180 per cent of their proportion of the general population 3 to 4 times that of White youth. Sixty per cent of juveniles in custody in public facilities were minorities (Allen-Hagen 1991), compared to 45% in 1977.

An article recent that appeared in *The Detroit News and Free Press* shows statistical numbers that link race to the type of crime and arrests. Blacks in Michigan have more arrests for assault, murder and drug offenses. Whites make up the greatest proportion of sex criminals, offenses against children, burglars and white-collar crimes. Crime costs America $425 billion a year, and prisons are **one of the biggest** industries in this country (Hoffman & Basheda, 1A+).

Fifty-six percent of Michigan's prison population is Black; 41% White, with other groups accounting for the remaining 3%. Whites commit serious and violent crimes at about the same rates as Black folks but are arrested, prosecuted and sentenced by the courts more rapidly than any other group. Jesse Jackson emphasized the inequality of convictions for cocaine possession. Five grams of crack equals 5 years in jail. Five pounds of powered cocaine equals probation. Ninety percent of all drug offenses are for crack possession, and 90% of the offenders are Black. White are more likely to have possession of powered cocaine because of the cost. Therefore, **Most Whites w a l k!**

The Center for Addiction and Substance Abuse at Columbia University estimate that substance abuse and addiction claim 500,000 lives a year and drain $250 billion from the health care system in this country (Leland, 54).

In Detroit there are advertisements for malt liquor, beer, and cigarettes on gigantic billboards throughout Black neighborhoods and even attached to the sides of the City's bus transportation system. The market for malt liquor (40 oz.) is virtually non-existent in the White suburbs. Oakland County, one of Wayne County's (Detroit's location) surrounding suburbs, has a county ordinance against the use of freeway and building billboard advertising (City Zoning Ordinances, Chapter #45).

Blacks are participating in plus blamed for their own destruction. In this country there seems to be a national tool chest holding a royal hammer that has hammered a certain PSYCHOLOGICAL MENTAL PROCESS leading to Black ignorance.

This hammer then drives nails into the bodies and minds of Black folks in the form of welfare, guns, drugs, and lack of education. These destruction tools have been purposely placed here ELIMINATION DRAWING BOARD. Readers, decode the system.

Black males face more competition than Black females in the area of employment. Since 1900, the Black women's labor force participation rate in this country was 40.7% and 33.6% for Whites. In 1970, 49.5% and 42.6%; in 1980, 53.2% and 51.2%; and in 1991 it was 57% for Black women.

Between the years of 1938-1942, President Franklin D. Roosevelt brought Black women into the Federal work force to fill clerical and professional job areas. Traditionally, White culture accepts Black females socially. They have been able to find jobs more readily than Black males. For that reason the Black male often perceives the Black female as having more power than he does. He feels, in turn, that she does not respect his manhood.

Again, this lack of respect the Black female has for the Black male goes back to slavery. The typical slave family was matriarchal in form. The mother's role was far more important than the father's. Whatever significance the family had at the time rested in the responsibilities belonging to women—cooking, cleaning, and taking care of the house. The husband was his wife's assistant, her companion, and her sex partner--her possession. Slave families were referred to as "mother and her children" without reference to a father.

Because of these conditions and the absence of legal marriages, the father's limited role, and lack of any reasonable economic significance, it is easy to see why slave families were so unstable (Huggins, Kilson, Fox, 125). The Black female has the capabilities and trained to be independent—in a sense—independent-dependent with the help of Mr. Welfare.

In 1990 there were about 3.4 million women, 374,000 men, and 7.7 million children under 18 receiving AFDC nation wide. Forty percent (40%) of AFDC child recipients are Black (Sklar, 22-31). In Michigan ADC-Aide to Dependent Children the Black female becomes the head-of-the-household. This cycle of families living on welfare may be in the fourth or fifth generation.

The Black male in the same socio-economic category does not have the same pitiful, meager oppressive means to support himself. This contributes to him having to seek other means of support. Lack of selfrespect and America's long-term unemployment of millions of Black men is directly linked to the shrinking numbers of Black men who are likely to consider themselves suitable for marriage (Marriott, 86).

Too often, self-respect comes in the form of being preoccupied with MATERIALISM. A person might resort to making himself forget his miseries by using drugs or doing illegal things. This deprivation of becoming a strong male model in the eyes of society further creates strains between the Black male and female.

Basing self-worth on materialism and bragging about how much it costs for material self-worth stems from poverty. By having the latest fashions, car, and jewelry the ego boosts way up there, and a sense of egotism creates itself. In the Black community there are infants wearing designer jeans, shoes, and diapers. You have probably seen male toddlers with one ear pierced, a hat turned backwards, and a gold chain. What are mothers saying to their children?

If we give children everything they want, what do they have to look forward to when they grow up? Some Blacks suffer from faulty cognition's about themselves and others when the latest fashions and expensive cars become the main objective in life.

Psychologists say that the underlying causes for a person's behavior stems from something that happened in childhood. As children, most Black parents did not have material wealth and want to shower their children with the things they never had.

Blacks spend $400 Billion a year on non-essential frivolous material goods. Blacks spend 6.6% of their income with Black businesses, and 93.4% among other ethnic groups. Blacks make up 12 - 13% of this country's population (so the statistics tell us--the more truthful figure is probably 30 - 33%) but buy 26% of all Cadillac's sold, 31% of the cosmetics, 35% of all soft drinks, 38% of the cigarettes, 39% of the liquor, and 40% of the music and movie tickets sold in this country (Source: Ashid A. Savage, *The Black Eye* April 1, 1995).

Black men carry over into adulthood unstable relationships suffered by the Black Race dating back to the time of slavery. Many younger men feel that the responsibilities connected with a serious relationship are burdens and history plus the going topic on talk shows currently have "steer clear" written in black and white all over the screen.

People today, especially Blacks, are very materialistic. Black people love to dress well and eat well. Blacks like to drive nice cars and wear expensive jewelry. The average person might think that Black people own jewelry stores with a secret passage connected to one of the National mints. Black women love to get manicures that include jewel studded nail tips and will spend a fortune on the latest hairstyles. Then the flaunting starts with material objects. In some instances, a college education is less attractive than trying to find out who is wearing the latest style of gym shoes and jeans.

Slavery created a matriarchal relationship status between Black men and women. Women are the stronger of the Black Race and carry the title "head-of-household" exaggerated by the American public. The hiring of Black females in the corporate world happens because they are less of a threat than the Black male. Black females have traditionally filled two (2) quotas--female/Black.

During the Civil Right's Movement of the 1960's, Black men assumed the "in charge" identity status. A true statement of "Black Power" was the **power** to have a White woman by his side. The Civil Right's Movement was a "middle class" Black movement. Middle class meant gaining the same status as it relates to schools, neighborhoods, employment, and recognition. It's only natural that Black middle class assimilation into mainstream White America would also mean having a White woman.

The Black female's traditional role has always been that of "the stronger" person in a relationship. The Black female's strong domineering personality leads the Black male to feel that she does not respect his MANHOOD.

Some young Black women shake those long, fake fingernails and gyrate those necks and heads (weave and extensions flying all over) talking about "what a man can do for her." This sometimes backfires and is a complete turn-off for the Black man who can find a PERFECT, PASSIVE White woman who will do anything to please her Black man.

CHAPTER 7 O J Simpson's Symbolism Lynching

OJ Simpson, Kobe Bryant, Tiger (Negrito) Woods with all of his toothas, and Michael Jackson were America's continual proof that broad grinning lapdogs exist in the 21st Century. If you don't know what a lapdog is, do some reading. America can illustrate to its populace Blacks have never stopped basking in the affection of their masters. Simpson stands before Mr. Supremacy submissively—head slightly bent—Armani suited and Bruno Magli shoed to receive the favors and affection of his masters. He is a comedic media figure for Caucasians with "up in-the-butt" funniness and jokes. He still doesn't realize his banishment from America. White folks will not accept his "not guilty" verdict and never will.

In July 1994, the OJ Simpson preliminary trial hearings saturated every national and local newspaper front page, magazine cover, and interrupted television daytime programming. Even the NBA Championship game was Pre-empted so that America could watch the Los Angeles Police Department (LAPD) apprehend a Black fallen hero in a sort of 1990's style symbolism lynching.

Television dramatically illustrated the effects with the famous fleeing white Bronco. It concluded on October 3, 1995, and referred to as OJ on the "Freeway to Freedom" in a white minivan after acquittal in the now famous "Trial of the Century."

Shortly after his arrest for the murders of Nicole Simpson and Ron Goldman *Time Magazine* cover photo of OJ Simpson was retouched dramatically using computer technology. Compared with the original LAPD mug shot of Simpson, the retouched photo painted Simpson as sinister and ultimately, guilty. *Time* magazine used racial stereotyping and altering constitutes a news item).
the news (since a photo After Simpson's acquittal,

National networks heralded the "not guilty" verdict as one of the most polarizing moments in this country's history.

Because the jury was majority Americans felt that the jury was **not deficient** and did **not** carry out the judicial process to convict Simpson. Seventy-five percent (75%) of all White Americans polled voiced the opinion that injustice-**not** justice was served. The people polled also stated that their faith in the legal system -- greatly reduced.

The Simpson trial provided the world with an open window to racism in the US. Now we can add Hurricane Katrina to that dirty window of iniquity. As America played the nut role, the world tuned in to watch the window without the window dressing.

A great many people said: "Why would a whole police force frame Simpson?" W H Y??? Why did King James and his translators make the characters in the Bible White with a European setting? Why were the White Southern fundamentalists (Evangelicals of the day) able to justify slavery by

the "Grace of God?" As late as 1964, Blacks from other countries were refused US citizenship. Why did the US Government use Black men in a syphilis experiment as recently as 1972? Rodney King was beat publicly by the LAPD—why? Why did Murray and Herrnstein write a book and link race with intelligence? Why did President George Bush ignore the victims of Hurricane Katrina for three days but rushed in the middle of the night to get legislation on the books to stop the Supreme Court to remove tubes from brain-dead "Feed Tube Woman?"
Black, White impartial but

Simpson was the Black trump card needed by the LAPD to prove to the world that the department was successful in restraining a Black man who had gotten too uppity. The **verdict** tampered with media **authority** attempting to show the world that White life is more precious than Black life.

When the Simpson trial started, it was clearly evident the LAPD were the ones on trial. Because of the Rodney King beating that occurred in March 1991, and the nexus to fatuous racial defecation, great measures proving the LAPD lived up to the reputation as the efficient and trustworthy men in blue supervened.

The jury of 9 Blacks, 2 Whites and 1 Hispanic were immediately accused of jury nullification or ignoring the evidence to send a broader message. White America felt a surge of outrage and refused to accept the juries' findings. According to White America, justice was mocked. The scenario—a Black was man fighting the system rigged against him.

The immediate response was for Whites to make it difficult for Black juries to acquit Black There was an immediate push for a amendment allowing "non-majority" verdicts of 10-2, as well as new proposals that would limit peremptory challenges permitting lawyers to exclude jurors on the basis of race (Close, 28).

The evidence presented by the defense held no credence in White America. White America thought that a limo driver's testimony, a barking dog and the fact that the jury reached a verdict after less than four hours of deliberation were the **only three details needed to convict** Simpson because Black folk's votes don't matter. The three issues alone held more credibility than tainted

DNA evidence and 1,105 exhibits.

During testimony Johnnie Cochran attacked former LAPD Detective Mark Fuhrman calling him a "genocidal defendants.

California racist" and comparing his character to Adolf Hitler. Hitler was dictator of Germany for 12 years (1933-1945) and started World War II and ravaged all of Europe.

Cochran said, "People didn't care so they didn't try to stop him." The comparison shocked many observers. Fred Goldman, Ronald Goldman's father muttered, "He shoves racism in front of everything." On the other hand, Goldman didn't say anything about Fuhrman's comments when he testified, "Niggers should be piled up and burned."

During his 1991 Senate confirmation hearings, Supreme Court Justice Clearance Thomas thought he was subjected to a high-tech lynching. Thomas, like Simpson, thought he had transcended all racial barriers. He had acclimated himself into White society with a White woman at the end of his arm, was moving in and out of Caucasian circles and had probably forgotten he had a Black face. He was in the White Social Mimicry Realm.

To the American Press Thomas was the **seddity** Negroid who married a White woman. What is worse— being married to a White woman or killing a White woman? Both offenses carry the same risks.

Both Thomas and Simpson played symbolic roles in an old fashioned American Lynching. They inherited the status of America's **"Whipping Boys."** Judges play a central role in America's political life. The Supreme Court is the highest court in the land and interprets the Constitution. Do you really think that the country could let Thomas sit on the "high court" without a **subliminal racial incident**? Thomas is another "lapdog."

Anita Hill played her role in the symbolic high tech Thomas lynching. Thomas sexually National attention preempting television programming and even Saturday cartoons. News anchors came on the network stations to explain to children that they would

Some believed her testimony that harassed her. The hearings drew not be seeing their regular Saturday cartoons. It was "history in the making" explained the commentators. YES! Train them when they are young and when they are older they won't depart from it!

Thomas probably dropped Hill after realizing he could have **full** self-actualization with a White woman. Hill was caught-up in a situation that showed faithfulness to the Master/Media **Elites/White-Sided** way of doing things. He was atop the **IDEAL pedestal.** He had traveled down a freeway to fairyland and was on the gateway to glory with his new White wife.

America beamed with the Simpson Civil Trial verdict jubilation, but the American Press is not through with Simpson. Whites want African-Americans to have the "Status of a **Disposable** Identity." Television is now the primary source of news for most Americans and has the ability to bring events to millions of viewers. Television itself may be the factor in determining events. (Alexander & Hansen, 15) The broadcast media has the power to determine events.

The Black woman is able to secure employment or some gain of monetary support more readily than the Black male even if income comes from welfare dependency. The Black woman is not a direct threat to a White man because the White man still possesses his superiority over all women both Black and White.

To tell the truth, White women are the only beings on Earth who can make the White man feel inadequate. If the White woman goes after a Black man, that in essence is telling the White man he is truly nothing and has become labeled a "little lower than the animals" from whence he has categorized all Black men.

Black men have the power to carry on a color line and cause White annihilation. By having a White woman the Black man has the power to shoot down the White man's ultimate imagined authority. But in the meantime, he following scenario is staunchly in place. Impoverishment has caused a deprivation of material goods in Black communities that causes the craving for expensive gym shoes, clothes, gold jewelry, and expensive cars. Because a large number of Black men have acquired the status symbol job, earned respect in the community, and conquered the White woman sexually, they seem to have forgotten the struggle that many Blacks face every day just to stay alive.

Money and education boosts individual selfimportance and self-esteem, but a White woman helps some Black men to evolve into another world set apart from their own Black existence. They no longer feel anger towards the system because the slavery thing is extinct and people like me should just go away, stop talking, and stop the lucid madness.

Flawed American Law did not work to hang the Nigger who married a White woman. What was worse in the media's eyesight—being married to a White woman or killing a White woman? It all boiled down to White men grasping at the only thing they had left—their ability to duplicate the Caucasian Race. White women at childbearing age represent 2% of the global population. The dwindling Caucasian birth rates are causing depopulation of Whites as they disappear from the face of the Earth.

CHAPTER 8 Desperately seeking fairyland Whiteness

It's not hard to explain my position. Television and movies consume American lives. Ninety-seven % of all homes in this country have at least one television and a VCR (Alexander & Hanson, 9). As the viewer flips through the hundreds of cable and commercial stations, there are not a lot of Black faces on the screen. Every where a person looks, the image of a White man can be seen from the average American, to the President, to God himself!

In turn, Black people can only identify with White faces, White verbal patterns, White family situations, and White historical programs on the PBS, History, and National Geographic Stations, a White God and White Mary on the religious stations, and only White heroes or just plain **WHITE DOMINATION**. We present White people to the viewer as the smartest, prettiest, strongest, purest, most innocent, and most divine people in the world.

White domination in this country has definite similarities to Ivan Pavlov's Classical Conditioning Learning by Association Experiment performed in

1927. **White** has been superimposed to mean higher in quality and merit by mass media; thus, emitting a reflective response producing the attitudes of White right! Black back!

Pavlov was the Russian physiologist who studied the role of saliva in digestion. To study the reflective response of the salivary glands to the presence of food in the mouth, he surgically implanted tubes in the cheeks of dogs so that saliva drained out. He precisely measured the salvia after the dogs ate small amounts of food.

White preeminence implantation -- psychologically into the psyche to produce a universal White footing/foundation. Pavlov accidentally discovered that after a few days the dogs he used in the experiment started salivating when the attendant entered the room with the food dish BEFORE food placed in their mouths. The sights and sounds of the attendant produced a reflective response that only the food had originally elicited (Lahey, 142).

Stated in a different way, the Black man witnesses a form of learning based on the repeated association with "WHITE ONLY." "WHITE DOMINATION" is the stimulus that directly influences conscious experience. Subconsciously the "WHITE ONLY" value system is directly linked to the Black man's sight and conscience and affects his behavior as he reaches manhood. After many years of repeated association with "WHITE ONLY" a reflective response has occurred, **but** many **Blacks** and **Whites** would **outright deny** such a thing has taken place because the writer should **STOP** practicing tribal identities.

The stimuli of "WHITE ONLY" elicit a response that results in a permanent change of behavior brought on through experience. The Black man is an outcast in society if he does not go with the White FLOW.

White people can only identify with other White people. That is the major cause for White flight from majority White cities, neighborhoods and schools. As a city, neighborhood, or school becomes half Black, White people start leaving in droves because they have lost their means of identification. Whites want to look around and see people who look the way they look.

Whites cannot incorporate Black perspectives— goals, actions, and values into their lives because of the separation realm that exists between groups of people who are different colors.

It has been easy for Blacks to assimilate into the White culture after years of rote indoctrination. The reverse is true for Whites who constantly tune in but watch different channels. **culturally dual** citizens.

If, for example, a department store and two clerks are present, one Black and the other White, the White person will look and talk directly to the White clerk as if the Black clerk were **not** even present.

The White patron does not give it a second thought because the White clerk is the person with which he can identify. This identification has become instinctive with most people and would **not** admit they were doing something wrong.

This identification process is just not evident with Whites only. On college campuses across the country, Blacks also separate themselves. Any college student union has Blacks on one side and Whites on the other.

The school district where through an integration process. 50% White, 40% Black, and 10% Latino. The district is now 70% Black, 20% White, and 10% Latino.

The Whites and Latinos have bonded themselves together as comrades. The Whites date Latinos and mingle together in groups because the two groups assimilate and band together to increase their numbers and representation.

Identification is important in the socializing process. Whites cannot incorporate or accept into their lives thinking, actions, and feelings unless the individual looks the same way they look. Right now Whites stand on Blacks are both Black/White

White person walks into a
employed has gone

The district was once their own ideal pedestal. Example: The next time you go to work pay attention to White people's conversations.

Whites pick and choose other White faces when making references to work place surroundings. Blacks are not referred to as part of the work place unless in a negative fashion. Blacks are manufactured beings. Years of indoctrination and training citizens of this country to develop refinement of intellectual and artistic taste based on White cultural values have created human beings who suffer from self-hate; in fact, some Blacks do not mind calling themselves "Nigger" casually.

Neighborhoods and schools are "good" if majority White, and "bad" when majority Black. Blacks use the same connotation when they refer to straight hair as good and kinky/nappy hair as bad. Large American cities populated by a Black majority are a result of the same good/bad thought process.

Blacks will **not** buy a house from another Black person as the neighborhood becomes integrated but **will** jump to buy from Whites as White Flight looms on the horizon. It is even hard to get Blacks to patronize a Black owned store.

IMAGINED ASSIMILATION ASSURES PSEUDO ACCEPTANCE

As a result of this behavioral classical conditioning, a spill over of self-hate and self-loathing has seeped into Black minds readily seen on the surface. Look around folks and you will see Black women who have dyed their hair every shade of blonde and red. Look closely at Black women with blue and green CONTACT eyes, and I am not talking about the Blacks in this country who have natural blonde hair and blue/green eyes. Beauty supply stores in Detroit, for example, stay well stocked with bleaching cream, long-flowing wigs in an assortment of colors, and hair dye featuring hues from jet black to *honey blonde.*

This pseudo-assimilation with the White Race raises self-esteem. The Black woman now sees herself as beautiful. When she looks in the mirror, she now appears Whiter to Mr. Mirror Image on the other side starring back at her. Mr. Mirror Image is telling her Mirror, Mirror on the wall, which's the fairest of them all—"That White woman with blonde hair and blue/green eyes!"

DESPERATELY SEEKING WHITENESS

Black women send messages to Black men help him hate how the women of his race look. When he sees his mother and sisters trying to change their looks to pseudo White, it makes him seek what the Black woman also sees as beautiful. Mr. White Supremacy has put his women high on the **IDEAL** pedestal.

Desiring self-actualization, the Black man feels that he can build his standards of self-worth by seeking the embellished White woman high atop the pedestal. ASSIMILATION ASSURES ACCEPTANCE in the minds of Blacks who feel they will be more readily accepted as a **whole** person if they can assimilate into the dominate culture of this country.

The Black man has internalized and perceived himself as worthwhile only when he acts and feels in accordance with the conditions that do not go against the WHITE grain. He often denies feelings that are inconsistent with the internalized conditions of worth and feels that the quest to DESPERATELY SEEK WHITENESS is the only way to be truly worthwhile. This ASSIMILATION ASSURES Caucasian ACCEPTANCE in his mode of building self esteem.

Asians don't walk around with dyed blonde hair because they are proud of their heritage. Their history and customs are in tact. They love the way they look and would not go to the same lengths to change their physical appearances.

In the late 1940's Kenneth and Mamie Clark conducted some psychological studies of self-image and self-evaluation. Black children given a choice to choose between Black and White dolls resulted in sixty-seven % (67%) of the Black children choosing White dolls.

In 1985, five decades later, the results of Derek and Darlene Hopsons' study were similar. Sixty-five percent of the Black children chose White dolls. Seventy-six percent (76%) said the dolls "looked bad" to them. They made comments that they were not as good, as pretty, or as nice as Whites.

After acknowledging racial issues, conducting positive modeling and reinforcement of Black images, only 35% of the Black children chose White dolls the second time (Frazier & Warner, pp 1+).

Noted psychologist AH Maslow studied selfactualization and related it to the humanistic approach. Self-actualization is the need to develop one's potential fully. White America will continue to practice tribal identities. It keeps America's Whites and Blacks confused and preserves the Browns as Caucasian.

THE GREATEST GIFT - ON THE FREEWAY TO Fairyland Whiteness

By marrying and having White women by their side, Black men have the mindset they are traveling down a freeway to fairyland or on a gateway to glory. His embellished White woman will help him psychologically share the top of the pedestal. Actually, he is traveling on the freeway to falsehood with a Geiger counter girth.

No matter how hard he tries, Mr. White Supremacy will topple him from atop his psychological pedestal. Just watch a Black man who has a White woman by his side. He walks a new walk and talks a new talk. His chest is stuck out, and his head held high as he struts his stuff

with his White baby doll.

IN THE STARTING GATE SEARCHING FOR THE BIG BRAWNY BLACK HUNK

The United States has always made race distinctions, and the Black Race has always had a fixation with color because of racial distinctions. This color fixation has sealed off part of the mind from developing a sense that Black is "REALLY OKAY!" The color fixation has divided the Black Race for decades. Some Black men feel that in order to be successful, he has to be seen with a light-skinned woman (Bates, 79-80).

The trend today seems to be that of relating success to having a White woman. A White woman psychologically equalizes a Black man and makes him think he has reached the **ideal**. handsome, aggressive, exciting, adorned than White men. For that reason Ms. White Thang wants one too.

In the midst of the Simpson hearings, Montel Williams, Jenny Jones, and Geraldo, aired show formats about White women and the Black men they seek. Talk shows in the early 1990's were on front and center stage in the average person's home. The talk shows provide American viewers with a simulated group therapy session, and if the viewer doesn't see it on Jerry Springer, he can see it on Maury Povich the following week.

After watching one show, a viewer who was on the verge of settling an issue just might have an answer. There are a lot of answers to societal questions in television land because of the saturation with talk shows and reality TV by the networks.
Black men are more and more sexually

The once popular talk shows have done their best to reinforce stereotypes. They make Blacks look like the most foolish people hostesses, panel, psychotherapy in groups. The topic for the day offers the panel and audience therapeutic experiences. The panel gets encouragement from the audience members.

People in groups can influence behavior. People act differently when they are in groups than when they are alone. History has shown that mobs commit crimes that individuals alone would not commit. Groups change behavior through diffusing responsibility and modeling (Lahey, 468). When behavior and attitudes are inconsistent, the attitudes often change to match the behavior. Media uses social situations to influence our behavior. Taunting your White women will only make them rush out of the starting gate in search of the brawny Black hunk. **You've tickled your White woman's fancy!**

on Earth. The talk show hosts, and audience actually conduct

CHAPTER 9 The Elimination Drawing Board (Historical Hidings)

Why are there so many disputes surrounding the origin of man or the existence of Black men in America? The discovery of Homo Erects occurred in Africa, but there still are many monumental objections and disputes related to the findings. Scientists want to prove that modern man originated in Russia or Asia--any place but Africa. The first erectus Olduvai Gorge, Tanzania.

A popular talk discussion/debate about teenage racism. One teenage White girl was very upset when a Black panelist said, "Jesus was a Jew." Her comment was, "Jesus was not a Jew." "He was a White Christian." Oh, how we have permeated the minds of our young people to believe falsehoods!

What would have happened if a panelist said that Abraham, Isaac, and Jacob, the original people of God and the original Jews were African/Edenic men? There would have been a riot on the set. The European concealment of ancient Afrocentric biblical traditions has led to a Biblical European setting. The Western world believes Christianity was the way to save the Black savages captured for slavery. King James and his crew would not accept Afrocentric traditions pre-designed.
fossil findings occurred in

show spotlighted a
Biblical & Historical Events you never learned in Sunday school

The Garden of Eden was ancient Cush translated into Anthiops, which was the former name of Ethiopia meaning Burnt Face People. In Antiquity, Africa was "The Land of Ham." The Hebrew were Cushite. The words "Middle East" and "Semitic" are both 19th Century cultivations by the European Academy. That is why people are appalled because history has linked the Biblical Old Testament to Africa.

God promised the land of Canaan to Abraham and his descendants (Genesis 12:1-7). In the Chapter 10 of Genesis, Canaan is the "Land of Promise." Canaan was also the fourth of Ham's sons. Ham, according to Webster's European Dictionary, is the father of the Black Race because his father cursed him in Genesis 10:25-6. Canaan (Ham) was cursed--a servant of servants unto his brethren. The Lord God blessed Shem and enlarged Japheth.

The name Ham (Cham/Kam) came from Egypt where Moses was born, grew up, and lived until the Exodus. The Egyptians called their country *Kemit* meaning "black" in the Egyptian Language. It is natural to find *Kam* in Hebrew, meaning heat, black, burned and helps to explain evidence of civilization in Black Africa (Diop, 7-8).

People actually believe that Canaan was cursed to become a servant to White people. If Greece invaded Egypt about 30 BC (there were probably very few if any White people in Egypt). So-called God-fearing people used the same theory to justify slavery in the 1600's, 1700's, and 1800's.

History tells you that the Egyptians settled Ethiopia." In the Bible it is wirtten that Mesraim, son of Ham, brother of Chus (Kush) the Ethiopian, and of Canaan, came from Mesopotamia to settle with his children on the banks of the Nile.

According to the King James Version of the Bible, Egypt's population contained the offspring of Ham, ancestor of Blacks: The descendants of Ham are Chus, Mesraim, Phut and Canaan. Note: Punt is now Uganda. The descendants of Chus are Saba, Hervila, Sabatha, Regma and Sabathacha. Chus was the father of Nimrod; he was the first to be conqueror on the Earth. Mestraim became the father of Ludim, Anamin, Laabim, Nephthuhim, Phethrusim, Chasluhim. Canaan became the father of Sid, his first-born, and Heth.

Mesraim still designates Egypt; Canaan, the entire coast of Palestine and Phoenicia; Sennar, which was probably the site from which Nimrod left for Western Asia, still indicates the Kingdom of Nubia. Noah and wife produced Shem and Japheth depicted as White by Europeans because Jewish today means "RELIGION" and "NOT RACE."

The ancestor of all Jews was Abram in Genesis, Chapter 12. Abram was an ancestor of Shem who was one of Noah's sons. Again, we go back to the same situation. Shem was the brother of Ham, supposedly the father of the Black Race. If Ham was Black, so were Noah and Shem, and Japeth, and so were the original Jews. That is the way it adds up.

The original Bible ended up translated from **Hebrew and Greek** into Latin, English, and other languages. The translations obviously sparked misinterpretations. The Bible mentions Ethiopia (Abyssinia) 40 times and Egypt over 100 times, but it never mentions Germany or England. In fact, Ethiopia and Egypt mentioned interchangeably (African Heritage Bible, x).

The descendants of Abraham, Isaac, and Jacob were African/Edenites, the original people of God. During biblical times **"Africa"** included much of what European maps today call the "Middle East" (African Heritage Bible, x).

The geographical designation the world known as the Middle East started after World War II. The term Middle East now includes Turkey, Greece, Iran, Ceylon, Burma, Cyprus, Syria, Lebanon, Iraq, Israel (Palestine) Jordan, Egypt, Sudan, Libya and the Arabia Proper.

European geographers divided the Middle East territorial mass into three sections based on the distance of each from **Europe**. The original Middle East is now the Near East, Middle East, and Far East (Encyclopedia Britannia, 644). Europe set up **the rules and regulations for this round**.

Completion of the King James translation in 1611, referenced Biblical Black people Biblical as Ethiopian **not** Negro, hoping the common minds of that day could not see Ethiopian as a color. Right now the US has classified all people from the "Middle East" as Caucasian— including Ethiopians. The color theory itself disputes Black people evolving from White people (African Heritage Bible, 3). White means absence of color. It is possible to get white from black because the color black contains the mixture of all colors.

Christ Jesus was Black. In Matthew 2:15 and Hosea 11:1 the words are found, "Out of Egypt, I have called my son." The verses relate to Mary and Joseph's hiding Jesus from King Herod.

Logic in play: During slavery run-away slaves in the US would have stuck out like a sore thumb because of their Black skin. If Mary and Joseph had been White in color, think about their chances of hiding from King Herod in **Africa.**

Most Christians today, as it has been for many centuries, accept that the Bible, Old and New Testaments is a complete compilation of their creed, of the doctrine of their Church and a true historical description of the life of Jesus Christ and of the events that were part of his life.

The King James Bible, for example, is a true anthology of the Christian doctrine. Both Old and New Testaments are anthologies of texts as ***chosen*** *literature*, but most of the Biblical doctrines -- left out. The Nicaea Council made the choice during the first centuries of the Christian era in AD 325. The religious authorities of that time made the choice of which books to include and which books to exclude from the Bible. The books ended up divided into three categories: accepted, disputed, and rejected.

The documents found in the last hundred years at Nag Hammadi and near the Dead Sea, as well as the deciphered Q Gospel, show clearly that the Bible does not give a true historical picture of Jesus Christ as an example. The scrolls of Qumrân have changed the understanding of events and circumstances mentioned in the New Testament.

Dead Sea documents showed that the Christian doctrine had nothing original and was from the Jewish Qumrân community. The Jordan Government forbids the export of the scrolls to many scientific foreign universities that had already paid for them. The universities reimbursed but the scrolls remained in Jerusalem that was part of Jordan at that time. The Palestine Archaeological Museum
International Board of
International Team fell
nationalized in 1966, its

Trustees dissolved, and the under the supervision of the Jordanian
Department of Antiquities (Hoover, Roy W.
Bible Books: Bible Review, Vol. ix, April 1993, p 44). THE FIRST
ROMANS AND GREEKS WERE
BLACK: The earliest known natives of Italy were
Negroes, thus making the base of the Latin Race is
Negroid. This based on observations of the earliest known
Etrurian pottery. The pottery includes examples of Etrusian vases molded in the forms of Negro heads, green in color, painted with Negroid characteristic features and woolly hair. Specimens of both preserved among the collections in the British Museum in London, England (Prehistoric Man, Vol. I, 269-70, London, 1876). THE NEGROID IN ANCIENT GREECE: The earliest Greek gods, like the Egyptian ones, were black. The Black man established the religion of ancient Greece, like that of Egypt. Not only were the Grecian gods black, but also Negroes, namely those of Dodona and Delphos, established

the two most important oracles of Greece. Two black doves that flew across the waters, from Egypt, the black doves being symbolic of black priestesses, founded the first, according to Herodotus.

He said also that the cries uttered in the Greek temples during the Hellenic rites sounded as if they had come from Africa (ref. Rogers, J. A. Sex and Race, VOL. I, 80, and The History of Herodotus, Book II, p. 100, copyright, 1928, by Dial Press, Inc., Tudor Publishing Company, 1947).

Sen Wosret I (1971 to 1927 B. C. E. "Before the Common Era") also known as King Kecrops was said by the Greeks to be the founder of the Greek city-state, ATHENS. This Egyptian power and influence included the Red Sea, up to as far as Punt.

It also included what today we call the Mediterranean, Libya, Israel (Palestine), Syria, Crete, the Aegean Islands, and even the mainland of Greece itself. Sen Wosret inherited this great legacy (ref. *Egypt Revisited*, Ivan Van Sertima, 1989, Dr. Asa Hilliard III, 218).

BLACK GODS AND MESSIAHS: The earliest gods and messiahs on all the continents were black. Research has yielded an impressive amount of material on the subject. The messiahs, some of whom lived many centuries before Christ, had lives that were closely parallel to Christ. Moreover, the word Christ comes from the Indian, Krishna or Chrishna, which means "The Black One" (ref. Rogers, J. A. Sex and Race, St. Petersburg, FL. H. M. Rogers, VOL. 1, 265).

The gods of antiquity from Greece to Mexico were black: Osiris and his Bull were black and all the Gods and Goddesses of Greece were black. That is true with Jupiter, Bacchus, Hercules, Apollo, and Ammon. Osiris and Isis were mythical heroes at one time. The discovery of Osiris' tomb linked him to being an initial ancestor of the Pharaohs. The Egyptians always painted their gods black as coal in the image of their race, just as Whites would have painted their gods white (Diop, 76-7). **THE STORY OF VANISHED NEGRO CIVILIZATIONS:** In his book African Glory, Dr. John Henrik Clarke, writes: The story of the Journey which Hanno, the Carthaginian, made along the north-west and the west coasts of Africa in about 520 BC with a fleet of sixty ships and a human complement of 30,000. Homer, (*Iliad* iii -1200 BC) describes a race of tiny folk dwelling in a far southern land, "Whither the cranes fly when inclement winters and piercing frosts visit the northern shores." Fierce battles mentioned by later writers occurred between the pygmies and cranes and represented on their vases and other art work. On vases, the pygmies are dwarfs with large heads; Negro features, close, curly hair, and sometimes armed (Druids and Leprechauns).

Aristotle firmly believed in the pygmies. He characterized them as a race of men with small stature inhabiting the marshes of Upper Egypt towards the sources of the Nile. Representations of the pygmies sculptured on tombs at Sakkarah refer to the V Dynasty of Egypt (3366 BC). The pygmies depicted in basrelief on these tombs faithfully reproduce the racial with lances

existence of characteristics of the present race of pygmies inhabiting the Ituri and Semliki Forests.

Niku (Necho) II, the last but three of the native Egyptian Pharaohs, commissioned a captain of the Phoenicians, whose ships stationed in the Gulf of Suez, to sail around the Continent of Africa. The early voyages along the west coast of Africa established the first links of that part of Africa with the early civilizations that were centered on the Mediterranean (ref. Clarke, Dr. John Henrik & deGraft-Johnson, J C African Glory, 1954, 17). Natives from Lebanon claim to be the original Phoenicians. People from the Middle East (Arabs) who have migrated to the US are historically a Negroid Race. The Phoenicians and Egyptians are ancient cousins.

The Cro-Magnon Man (a race extinct for 10,000 years) links to Black Africans through archeological measurements in size and stature. The BushmenHottentots population of South Africa suffers from a morphological characteristic derived from a deformation of the spinal column at the level of the hips. The slope of the pelvis and steatopygia linked to the now extinct man exists in the Black Race and some Brown Races (Reclassification for Falsification).

Scientists refer to the Negroid Race as the "Sicklecell Race," but the disease appears wherever people have to cope with prolonged exposures to malaria. Sickle cell is as prevalent in parts of Greece, South Asia and Central Africa. Is Sickle cell prevalent in people with Negroid blood?

The theory that physical characteristics most people associate with race are the result of adaptations to climate and diet but not an admixture with original man seems pretty far-fetched. Scientists have determined that there is no homogeneous race because inherited traits do not cluster and do not stay within any particular group.

The following examples cited are true examples of a pseudo-scientific theory used in our Encyclopedias, reference books, and history books for years. According to one author, if skin color determines race, the Dravidians (from Sri Lankan/Ceylon on the tip of India) are lumped with the Negroid Race. If we go by hair form, the Dravidians are lumped with the Europeans. If we classify men by height and shape of head, the Nordic peoples fall in the same group as many Negro tribes, and the Mediterranean people grouped with the Negro tribes of Africa.

There are people who are only **moderately** (meaning indistinct) dark-skinned, or who have hair that is only slightly wavy or **slightly kinky** (slightly meaning indistinct). To the Author is seems like the men who wrote this particular book are pulling an outright bamboozlement on the general public or an outright insult of the reader's intelligence.

• On the Southeastward Italian peninsula, people with black hair and dark eyes prevail. The further south you go the skin **becomes darker** (meaning indistinct). According to this same author, in Sicily, the people are dark-complexioned, but the Sicilians
-- not considered Black.

• In Egypt the people are **darker-skinned than** (meaning indistinct) the Sicilians -- not considered as Black.

• In the Seventh Century, Arab armies North Africa, converting the **Berber** considers Berbers Caucasian.) natives Mohammedan religion. These Arabs stayed and **interbred**, but the Arabs not considered Black.

• In the Eighth Century an army of Moors (consisting mostly of Berbers) invaded and conquered Spain. The ancient Berber was the brown Libyan, but invaded

(Webster to the Berbers are of Egyptian ancestry. They remained in parts of Spain for nearly 800 years. The Modern Spaniard has some Moorish heritage (Boyd, 30). The Spanish soldiers who had Moorish heritage tried to invade England in 1588 but failed. They ended up in Ireland where they remained and **interbred** in Ireland, but these people not considered Black.

• A Hindu may have dark skin like a Negro but will possess none of the other Negro characteristics hair, bone structure and **not usually considered a Negro** (meaning indistinct).

• An Irish European may have thick lips, or quite kinky hair, or a broad snub nose and yet not considered Black because his skin is **not dark enough**. The Moors also invaded Ireland just as they did in Spain and Italy. In Paragraph 5, the Hindu has dark skin like a Negro but not considered Black. So Paragraph 6 is **double-talk**.

• The Aborigines described in the Encyclopedia Britannia as black/dark brown chocolate in color with deep-set eyes and large protruding broad noses, which look just, like the HottentotsBushman of Africa. Their hair ranges from curly to frizzy but considered members of the White Race and listed as Caucasians. Aboriginal means existing from the beginning. The earliest known inhabitant; a primitive people to which all White men must establish linkage because he is the first/and or original, and everything came from him.

• The New Guinea Islands, 95 miles north of Australia, contains people referred to as Oceanic Negroes by the Encyclopedia Britannia. The settlers came there about 3000 BC. From these islands the people migrated to the islands of Fiji, Samoa, and Tonga. Around AD 500, they migrated to Hawaii.

• People in the Southwest Pacific Islands, Hawaiians and Samoans like the Aboriginal of Australia have long kinky hair and have black/dark brown skin. They are like the Maoris of New Zealand and **not** considered Black even though they migrated from Oceania 95 miles away where the people carry the classification of Oceanic Negroes.

NOTE: Get the point! Sift through the rhetoric. The author is referring to a distance of less than 100 miles. Clean it up! It's dirty! It is a big fat lie!

1. Sri Lankan/Ceylon, home of the Dravidians who interracially mixed with the Moors in that country. Ceylon is an island located off the southern tip of India.

2. Arabia contains people who are light to medium brown -- considered White. In the year AD 711 Moors crossed the Strait of Gibraltar and marched into Spain. They remained in Spain until driven out in 1492.

3. Most of the people of India are a blend of two early groups of people, the Dravidians (Moors) and the Aryans. A Moor is a Berber. A Berber is a member of ethnic groups in Northern and Eastern Africa including the ancient Egyptians, Coptic (Abyssinia) and/or Ethiopian, a descendent of Ham. Black people in the United States are a variety of colors which also includes different colors of hair and eyes—from white skin to blue eyes from Brown skin to brown eyes.

There were two types of Negroid that existed on earth in ancient Egypt, the straight-haired Dravidian and the woolly-haired Negro. Negro blood ethnology validated by scientifically cleansing mummies of that time period using ultraviolet rays to determine the amount of melanin in pigmentation. The difference between White and Black in this respect is the fact that the Black organism does not secrete any enzymes to absorb melanin the subsistence that produces dark skin.

The White organism does absorb melanin. The epidermis exactly like that of all other African Blacks. It is true of all the ancient Egyptians. Therefore, Egyptian mummies have remained Negro (Diop, 237). The Black Indian Dravidian groups regarded as as Caucasian-by-Caucasian scientists.

Negroid human substrata are extensive in many parts of the world including North Italy, North Portugal, Spain (west of the Pyrenees) and other scattered places in Europe. This same type of brown race existed among the ancient Neolithic inhabitants of the British Isles, France, and on both shores of the Mediterranean, throughout the Arabian Peninsula and on the coasts of the Persian Gulf.

The Yellow Race as well was the result of crossbreeding between Blacks and Whites at a very ancient time in the history of mankind. The ethnic features of yellow people—lips, nose prognathism, are those of the mixed breed. Their high cheekbones, puffed eyelids, Mongolian pucker, slant eyes, and depression at the bridge of the nose could merely result from the effect of thousands of years in a climate that blows cold winds on the face. These

features change from northern to southern Asia, following to some extent a climatic curve. Wherever there are yellow-skinned peoples, one still finds small pockets of Blacks and Whites who seem to be the residual elements of the race.
secrete enzymes to appears pigmented

This is the case throughout Southeast Asia: The Mois in the mountains of Vietnam have names like Kha, Thai, and Cham; like the Negritos and Anius in Japan. According to the Japanese proverb, For a Samurai to be brave, he must have a bit of Black blood.

Chinese chronicles report that a Negro empire existed in the south of China at the dawn of the country's history (Diop, 280-1). There are pyramids in China (Pyramid Valley) larger than the pyramids in Egypt.

The pyramids are off limits to outsiders. The Great Pyramid in Egypt is in alignment with the Pyramid of the Sun in Teotihuacan, Mexico. People of color are the only group of people who built pyramids in the world (BoyerLarkin, 1-C).

The probability of encountering men with black skin and woolly hair without any other ethnic feature common to Negroes is scientifically null and void. For a scientist to call such individuals "Whites with black skin" is as absurd as the appellation "Negroes with white skin" (Diop, 288). People of the world who are deep chocolate brown in color with curly or kinky hair are not part of the Caucasian Race. This has to be termed a pseudo-scientific theory. Do it to dispute the African origin of man and hide the Black conquest of the world?

Sir Isaac Newton discovered the color spectrum. The theory presents solid **proof** that Black came first. Newton was an English physicist who took a glass prism and passed a beam of sunlight through it. When the light passed through the prism, it formed a rainbow he later called the color spectrum. Although people can see six or seven colors in the spectrum, there are only three basic colors. The primary colors are red, yellow, and blue.

By mixing the three primary colors of red, blue, and yellow together, the color Black produces. Black is the color from which all other colors materialize and is dominant. White, on the other hand, is the color of maximal lightness from which no other colors are produced and is recessive.

A little every day thing like Isaac Newton's discovery of the color spectrum shows more validity as it points to an African origin than the many years of research and long drawn out scientific theories to disparage and dismiss Black cultures and history. While scientists interpret, record, and test their theories, all they need is a small box of Crayola Crayons containing eight crayons and a sheet of paper to prove the KEY TO THE COLORS. White is a recessive color, but Caucasians have shown a **dominant** upper hand.

In 1775 Johann Friedrick Blumenback, a German anatomist, established a racial classification system. He is the scientist who named the European Race Caucasian, the supposed superior beauty of people from this region. He then attached this aesthetic criterion to the basis of a scientific judgment about place of origin (Gould, 66). The Color Theory proves that it is possible to create all colors from black; whereas, it is impossible to create none from white. Does this also prove **HOW A RECESSIVE GENE SEEMS TO DISAPPEAR WHEN CROSSED WITH A DOMINANT GENE**?

Eye color genes are good examples to use. **Note: Blue eyes mean absence of pigment.** There is no such thing as blue pigment in the eyes. Blue eye color is a reflection just like water in a lake or the edge of a snow bank appearing blue in color. Genes control enzymes and also control the nature of physical characteristics in humans. Whenever two genes are identical, the person is homozygous for that characteristic. He has two browneye genes or two blue-eye genes. Whenever the person has different members of the particular gene series, he may possess the brown-eye gene on one chromosome and the blue-eye gene on its twin. The person is heterozygous.

When a person possesses two different genes for some physical characteristic at corresponding points of a pair of chromosomes, and only one gene seems to show, that gene dominant. The gene, which does not show, is recessive. In the case of eye color, the gene for brown eyes is dominant over the gene for blue eyes. The gene for blue eyes is recessive toward the gene for brown eyes (Boyd, 88-89).

We have been led to believe that Black history started in 1641 when slavery became a recognized statutory in this country. French explorer Henri Lhote discovered rock paintings showing Egyptians as Negroid before 3000 BC (Bennett, 4).

The Egyptians saw themselves as black, reddishbrown, and yellow. They used the color white to portray blue-eyed, white-skinned foreigners. The mural of a procession from the Tombe of Thebes in the time of Thatmes III shows 37 Whites who were White slaves to the King of Ethiopia (Bennett, 7).

Cleopatra, the sister of Alexander the Great of Macedonia who married Ptolemy V, King of Egypt, was enacted by Claudette Colbert in the (1934 DeMille) film version and Elizabeth Taylor (1963). Both actresses depicted the character of Cleopatra as a White woman. WHAT A MISCONCEPTION.

Scientists made a systematic examination of the skeletal remains of the ancient Egyptians and said Negroid people embodiment figured heavily in the PreDynastic Period. The Negroid element amounted to 42 per cent during the Middle Kingdom—11th, 12th, and 13th dynasties of Egyptian history (Bennett, 10). Encyclopedias and reference books refer to Egyptians as members of the Caucasian Race. The pages of reference books that line our library shelves revere the entire world as White.

In Egyptian history Ra Nehesi and several other Pharaohs identified as Black. So was Queen Nefertari, the most venerated figure. She was married to Aahmes I, Egypt's great imperial leader, who was co-founder of the famous 18th Dynasty.

In 1492 there were 80 - 100 million Aboriginal (Indians) in the Americas. By the end of the Century there were only 10 million left. Many Indian tribes have become extinct because of the European conquest. Europeans customs,
considered

manners,

Indians savages because their and religious beliefs deemed unfit/barbaric. The Congress of the US promised to respect the sovereignty and land rights of the Aboriginal. From 1790 to 1870, the US signed 371 treaties but broke every treaty it signed.

In his book, They Came Before Columbus, Ivan Sertima proves that Africans from Guinea came to the Americas before Columbus. Excavations in Mexico have unveiled a large number of Negroid heads in clay, gold, copper, and copal sculpted by pre-Columbian American artists. The strata on these heads ranged from the earliest American civilizations right through to the Colombian contact period.

US history fails to tell you that documentation by Ivan Van Sertima references ancient Africans using a secret trade route and arrived in the Americas 100 years before Columbus. The identification linking the collections to the Negroid Race were coloration's, fullness of lip, tattoo markings, beards, kinky hair, generously fleshed noses, and in some instances, identifiable coiffures, helmets, and compound earrings.

Frederick Pohl writes about archaeological remains (mysterious hieroglyphics) found in northern New York in his book Atlantic Crossings Before Columbus. The findings occurred before the arrivals of Leif Erickson and Christopher Columbus.

Not all Americans with African Ancestry walked off a slave ship starting in the 1600s. American history books have it recorded that Native American Tribes housed "runaway slaves" and that is why some Native American Tribes have Black faces.

In 1993, the United Nations Center for Human Rights recognized the Washitaw de Dugdahmoundyah Muur Empire as the Oldest Indigenous group of people on Earth. The registered Project # 215/93 ensued. Americans live under an ideological part of American Revisionist History. The following undermines the whole breadth and depth of the American history books.

The United Nations recognizes the Washitaw Muurs Nation within the United States along with the other Indigenous people of America. The Declaration on Rights of Indigenous People includes the Washitaw Nation-- Black People who have the archaeological and historical evidence to prove that the original inhabitants of North and South America (so called "Indians") were Black People who came here from Africa. Have you been to a Powwow and astonished at all of the Black Native Americans? The powwows attended were in Michigan and Ohio. Those Native Americans did not harbor runaway slaves which led me to believe the following: Black Indians are not solely a result of African slaves mixing with so-called Red Indians who were fleeing from slavery as many documented sources would have you to believe. Black Indians are indigenous to America—North, South, and Central before the so-called Red Man, before the Europeans, before the so-called Bering Strait crossings. The Olmecs, Washitaw, Moors, Yamasee, Mound Builders planted the seed of civilization in the Americas—Black Indians!"

The Mandingoes of the Mali and Songhay African Empires crossed the Atlantic Ocean in the 1300s (1324) to carry on trade with the Western Hemisphere Native Americans and further succeeded in establishing colonies throughout the Americas—both North and South America. Due to diplomatic relations with Morocco, the Malian emperor Sakura (AD 1285-1300) learned of advanced maritime techniques and the spherical nature of the Earth. Various Arab writers (Abdul-feda, Idrisi, Masudi, Abu Zaid, and Istakhri) developed geographies and formulated astronomical theories of those times.

The Negroid archaeological remains found in Mexico and New York are merely a basis or proof that Blacks sailed to the Americas in 1311 and settled when Columbus arrived in 1492. Black Native Americans still exist and existed before slavery.

Western scholarship/White scholars hotly dispute Black achievement. Napoleon Bonaparte, for example, made one cover-up, in the late 1700's. All of the history books in the United States revere Napoleon as one of the greatest rulers since Roman times. What's made visible in textbooks for all to see is a map HIGHLIGHTING Napoleon's European dominations showing control of the great **WESTERN WHITE CIVILIZATION** (Jantzen, Krieger, Neill, 461).

King James and his group of translators completed the **European Bible** in 1611 representing the first coverup of Black Origin/Achievement in modern history. Napoleon was also instrumental in helping to create cover-ups of Black Origin/Achievement.

The Great Sphinx built around 2559-2556 BC by ruler Chephren was thought to be defaced LITERALLY by Napoleon Bonaparte and his men in 1797. When Napoleon looked at the Pyramids and Great Sphinx of Egypt and saw

Negroid features, he ordered his men to shoot off their noses and lips. The Sphinx of Gize is definitely Negroid. It has to be because of the features the profile is rarely if ever shown in textbooks. The average person probably thinks that distortions in the pictures and books of the Pyramids are due to age deterioration. This is just another attempt to cover up African history and the origin of Egyptians.

The history books in the United States tell us that between the years of 1800 - 1810, Napoleon built Europe's greatest empire since Roman times. His victories over the Third Coalition gave him mastery in most of Europe with the exception of Britain, Russia, Sweden, and the Ottoman Empire. There are illustrations of world maps showing Napoleon's domination of the world SHADED in red.

The history books don't tell you that Napoleon Bonaparte imitated, taunted, Toussaint Louverture and defeated by Louverture's army. Louverture was the military leader, governor, and administrator of St. Domingo in 1799. He had been a slave for 47 years out of the 59 years of his existence. Toussaint's army and yearly revenue were larger in St. Domingo (West Indies) than any European power of the second rank.

The two principal cities of the colony were Cape Francais and Port Republican (Port-au-Prince), the Haiti we know today. Because Toussaint defeated Napoleon's army, he literally helped the United States acquire the Louisiana Territory. Because of Napoleon's defeat he lost interest in the Louisiana Territory and sold it to Jefferson.

The Louisiana Territory was no longer a French Colony but became part of the United States (Korngold, xiii). Negroes came with Columbus on his fourth voyage to the Americas in 1502. Hernando Cortez, conqueror of Mexico made use of slaves in hauling artillery to terrify the Aztecs (Quarles, 24).

In August 1619, more than a year before the landing of the Mayflower, a ship commanded by an Englishman anchored in the river off Jamestown in the colony of Virginia brought 20 Negroes counted as part of its cargo (Logan & Cohen, 1). Not only is ancient history distorted modern day American history fails to account for the many misconceptions. Americans probably think that

John Wayne, not the Buffalo Soldiers, settled the West and people like James Beckwourth. In 1950, on the 100th anniversary of the discovery of Beckwourth Pass through the Sierra Nevada Range, Universal International produced its Technicolor classic *Tomahawk* featuring a White actor Jack Oakie as the Black frontiersman James Beckwourth. Audiences learned Beckwourth was important but not that he was Black (Katz, 316).

Bulldogging or steer wrestling (downing an animal by biting its upper lip) is one of the seven standard events in present-day rodeos invented by Bill Pickett (a Black man). The earliest account of Bill Pickett recounted by Mexico's major newspaper, *El Diavio*, on December 24, 1908. There were also articles written about Pickett by a Tulsa World Newspaper reporter on October 11, 1931, of his many famous exploits. It staunchly stands that many stories about American Blacks, Indians, and others who are non-white have been buried (Hanes, xi).

Black Soldiers made up 9% of the enlisted men in the Army between 1866 and 1891. These regiments campaigned on the Great Plains along the Rio Grande, New Mexico, Arizona, Colorado, and the Dakotas that helped settle the West and helped connect telegraph wires in the West (Leckie, vii). Black Regiments after during and after World War II helped did the construction for the Alaskan Railway System but **not** mentioned in US history books used in the public school system.

CHAPTER 10 Black Functional Inferiority (creationism)

Blacks are the victims trawled to the Earth by the tools of inferior education, economics, and brainwashing. The White man has mastered the means to control. Slavery used historically and currently on a strategic level by the White man as a means to rein supreme. Think about the strategy of popular board and table games children and grownups have in their homes, and the point is indisputable.

Authors writing about race issues probably have used the same examples hundreds of times as introductions to their books. After the release of James Brown's music, *I'm Black and I'm Proud* (1968), many interesting brainwashing tactics surfaced in Black publications. The tactics mentioned again and again to show how White America has practiced **reinforced Black inferiority,** and how conditioning the subconscious to think and behave without conscious awareness.

Concealed Inferiority: In chess the White King moves first. The objective of the game is for the White King and Queen, plus all of the white pieces to move in a strategic pattern against all of the black pieces for the player to be victorious.

In Checkers the Black man moves last.
In billiards, if the black ball in knocked in a pocket, the player loses.
In the game Othello the player wins if he gets the white pieces to jump the black pieces.

Get the point! Blacks always come up on the short of the stick! Whites always feel that they are in control.

Whites use the word minority as a tool or checkmate to rein supreme. Whites are a minority in the world—not people with Black and Brown skin. Webster's Dictionary defines the word Black and White to represent evil vs. good. Read the following examples of the words black and white in retrospect and you will get the full jest of the definition whitewashed.

Black - Something that is dirty and bad--a black day or a black lie.
White - Pure and good

White Lie - A polite or harmless lie.
Black Lie - A heinous or harmful lie.

White List - a list of members of diplomats who are entitled to diplomatic immunity from the jurisdiction of the courts. **Black List** - A list of persons, corporations, or groups deserve punishment, blame, or suspicion.

White Knight - A political reformer or champion.
Blackguard - A scoundrel
Angel Food - White Cake
Devil's Food - Chocolate Cake

White Mans' Burden - Coined in 1899) from: Sea to Sea Rudyard Kipling--It means the assumed duty of the Caucasian Race to care for, educate, and govern underdeveloped and uncivilized countries like Africa and Asia.

Black Ball - A vote against
Black List - List of persons believed to deserve blame and suspicion

Blackmail - Trying to get money from someone by using a

threat
Black Mark - Selling of goods at unlawful prices or unlawful quantities.
Black Spot - An area of economic depression.
Black Mass - A travesty of the Christian mass ascribed to worshippers of Satan.
Black Sheep - A discreditable member of an otherwise respectable group.
Black Market - Using illegal means to buy a product or smuggling goods and services illegally.

White neighborhoods and schools-- referred to as "good." Black neighborhoods and schools -- referred to as "bad." Black colleges -- referred to as "inferior". Straight hair -- considered "good hair." Nappy hair -- considered "bad hair." Light skin -- considered "fair skin."

In the 1950's and 1960's, Crayola Crayons marketed a crayon called "flesh" that was a sort of pinkish tan. While in grade school, I could never understand why this crayon was in the box with the others, but now it is clear. The crayons sold nationwide to influence all children's minds. Children of that era were reinforced and reinforced and reinforces with every coloring book page.

As we used our Crayola Crayons and colored pictures in class, the teacher encouraged us to use the "skin color" crayon to color the paper/ink images of people in our coloring books and teacher provided workbook pages with the "flesh" color. We, therefore, surmised that the pinkish-peach "skin color crayon" was the preferred color of man.

Fugitives from Haiti are turned away, placed in holding areas in Florida, and sent back to Haiti because they do not meet the Cuban criteria Cuban. Cubans can stay in the US because of the "Wet Foot, Dry Foot Policy. In the 1980's fugitives from Vietnam and Cambodia were WELCOMED WITH OPEN ARMS.

In 1924, the United States Immigration Act excluded Blacks of African decent from entering the country but encouraged the immigration of Northern and Western Europeans. The Immigration Act of 1965 eliminated the national-origins quota system. Under the quota system, in effect since 1924, policy discriminated against Asians, Africans, and Southern and Eastern Eastern year effort by ethnic groups to eliminate race and ancestry as the basis for American immigration (Plano & Greenber, 1982).

Newsweek predicted that by the year 2010 Hispanics will be the largest ethnic group in this country—AND THEY ARE. The magazine did not tell you that 40% of all Hispanics have African ancestry. In the US, Latinos are neither a race nor an ethnic group and carry the classification of White (*Michigan Chronicle*, Aug 7, 1995). If Latinos are neither a race nor an ethnic group, and 85% of all Hispanics are classified as White, Latinos entering the US are already be passed off as an **extension of the White Race**-and have become comrades to build numbers even though they have a higher percentage of **Negroid blood than do most Black Americans.**

In 1808 there were three times as many slaves in Latin America than the Thirteen Colonies. Latinos represent a collection of nationalities descended from Europeans, African slaves, and American Indians. In America 80% of the current Black population have the same racial mixed derivations of Mexico, Central America and are considered Black, while those same people migrating to the US from the Mexico and Central American locations carry the classification Caucasian.

The French, Spanish, and British took more than 90% of the 10 million enslaved Africans to South and Central America and the Caribbean. Only 4.6% of the slave ships entered US waters. By 1793 colonial Mexico had a population of 370,000 Africans the largest concentration in all of Spanish America. In the United States there is only one division line Black/White, and the Latino immigrants entering the country do not understand that division.

Two sisters (biologically speaking) from Puerto Rico with brown skin and nappy hair were enrolled in my adult education class in suburban Detroit. They always spoke to each other in Spanish. One night they called me over to the table where they were sitting and asked, "What is your nationality?" I said that I was Black just like they were. They were appalled and started hollering, "We aren't Black." "We're Puerto Rican." I asked them if they had looked in the mirror recently. I said, "My skin is whiter than yours, and my hair is straighter than yours, but in this country I am considered Black."

In Puerto Rico people of Black, White, and Spanish descent exist, but in America considered Black women. They finally agreed with me but did not want that classification because of the negative image/impressions created in the US. The two sisters did not understand the importance that race has in this country and labeling meant nothing to them.

The Black female's traditional role has always been that of the stronger person in a relationship. The Black female's strong domineering personality leads the Black male to feel that she does not respect his MANHOOD. Some young Black women shake those long, fake fingernails and gyrate the necks and heads (weave flying all over) talking about "what a man can do for her." This sometimes backfires and is a complete turn-off for the Black man who can find a PERFECT, PASSIVE White woman who will do anything to please her Black man.

Why should the Black man finance a romance when he can romance without finance? While young Black women want payment for their companionship, White women who have never been able to find a man has her pick and may not her as materialistic. She is so grateful and will accept the attention **without** the currency. Some women actually believe that if a male friend does not provide her with material things, she does not want to be bothered.

Black men are so happy to have a White woman they will do anything to keep them. The first thing he does is treat them like queens and praises the very ground they stand on. Their every walk is like walking on holy ground, and their every talk is as if an angel were speaking.

The fat or ugly or low social strata, career diner waitresses and public display White woman, who has never received this kind of wholesome attention from a White man, eats up the attention.

The attention raises the White woman's selfesteem. She in turn gives the Black man all of the praise and attention he needs to make him feel like he is a REAL MAN. He automatically goes through an evolvement that puts him on the same notch as the superior White man.

The Black man has learned self-hate and loathing. He has also learned to hate the domineering Black woman because the passive White woman raises his selfesteem. Passive, submissive and supportive White women may only possess those three qualities, but will be crowned Queen for life. No matter what the Black man does, she supports and trusts him. He, in turn, feels he has one of the biggest white diamonds on Earth. Even the Black woman with the **Anti-Black** attitude sporting bleached blonde hair, weaves, and blue/green contacts can't compete.

Black men do not look beyond the superficial. Men want women who are beautiful, and to them beautiful is WHITE. The White woman is socially correct, socially astute, and she has it going on!!! The Black woman cannot compete no matter the price. The psychological surgeon has cut-the-cut and has artistically surged the surgery.

The Black man now has a White woman and feels that he is just as good as any White man in our White man dominated culture. He has the professional job, big house in the suburban community, and beautiful mulatto children so that he may assimilate into the White culture to assume PSYCHOLOGICAL EQUALIZATION.

Black women with bleached blonde hair, weaves, and blue/green contacts can't compete but are helping the **denial-Black** racial situation that exists in the Black community. If you feel that the blonde hair and blue eyes look natural, look close in the mirror. It will scare you-those growing dark roots and black circles that outline the blue glass stuck in your eye.

The movie *The Godfather* (1972) a Paramount film and pay close attention to the scene when Don Vita Corleone (Marlon Brando) talks about purposely planting drugs in the Black community. This move by the writer/director, fictionalized a bit for entertainment purposes, but the point -- well taken. Don Vita Corleone even makes a statement that it okay to place drugs for in the Black community because Blacks have no souls. There must be some truth to it. Crack Cocaine has replaced marijuana and heroine from the 1930's in the 1990's, which is just another method of CRACKING the BLACK man's whole being. *The Godfather's* setting was the 1930's, but 60 years later drugs have infiltrated the White community. The Mafia Dynasty probably did not realize that drug infiltration would also spread to include Whites.

Panther (1995) a Gramercy film also suggests that drugs saturated the Black community through underworld associations and the FBI. In the 1970's, the Black Panthers were infiltrated by the FBI and J. Edgar Hoover.

Between the years of 1865 and 1890, physicians believed that Black people were more susceptible to syphilis than Whites. The medical community attributed syphilis to Blacks because of involvement in rampant immorality and extreme ignorance. During that time, syphilis was perceived as an African American disease the Black Race brought upon itself. Was this the justification needed by the US government to conduct the Tuskegee Study?

Burundi, Central African Republic, Rwanda, Tanzania, Uganda, Zaire, and Zambia -heavily referenced.
LABELS for
The African countries
AIDS. In Sub-Sahara
have become the Africa six million

adults ended up infected with HIV. In all of Africa, most of the half-million babies born with AIDS have died (Neesday, 10-E).

In 1492 there were 100 million American Natives. In 1975 there were 500,000 American Natives left. This represents .5% of the indigenous people on the brink of extinction. In 1837, germ warfare in the form smallpox and measles were *whored* on American Natives. Syphilis misdiagnosed as leprosy (African American Encyclopedia, Vol. 6, 1540-1)?

In January of 1994, an article appeared in the *Albuquerque Journal* (10E) giving a detailed account of non-sterile medical applications. The author, Laurie Garrett Neesday writes: Doctors went into African countries attempting to vaccinate a population against various diseases and used the same disposable plastic syringes over and over again because the syringes were in short supply and reused. If doctors take an Oath of Ethics, how does something like this happen?

Most scientific journals try to prove that the HIV virus originated in monkeys and then spread to humans. Green monkeys in West Africa carry the disease SIVSimian Immunodeficiency Virus that is similar to the human HIV virus. Scientists cite many theories that have evolved as ancestors to the AIDS Virus.

NBC's *First Edition* reported in the mid 1990's that the station plans to do a made for TV movie about the production of deadly diseases in laboratories in the US. It plans to warn the general population about the possibility that diseases could spread through the population as a result of poor security at these scientific research facilities.

White couples take fertility drugs. According to the National Center for Health Statistics in 1997, there has been a remarkable rise in the number of multiple births over the past two decades. There were 1,034 multiple births in 1971 compared to 4,973 in 1995.

States reporting the highest ratios of multiple births are in Massachusetts, New Hampshire, New Jersey and Iowa. White women take fertility drugs to conceive because their men have turned into **habitual blank shooters.** Infertility and problems to conceive seem to thwart Whites more than any other race of people.

The Black male is a manufactured being. The media has a cue card for crime, a cue card for drugs, and a cue card for anger it flashes every time it wants to link a predicable action with a Black face. The manufactured Black anger festers into violent confrontations causing Black men to slaughter each other. Cracking the Black man's whole being has been successful. How many people do you know who believe: White's Right--Black Back!!! Education is the key to squelch the anger.

In his book Black Odyssey, Nathan Huggins outlines the truth of creating US history. He states . . . Race has become a shroud of social death. Black people do not exist in the world that matters. Revisionist history writes in a Master narrative. The language of the Constitution deals with the issue of slavery by writing the Three-Fifths Compromise. Nowhere else in our Constitution are slaves and Blacks mentioned (*Preface*).

Charter schools--heralded as the main ingredient for educational reform in the US to promote student quality performance. The underlying reason for creating charter schools is to break up the public school system, as we know it makes Blacks incapable of running American urban school systems, and urban schools put back into the hands of the White State Superintendents.

Right now our public schools will serve as holding areas until the student has graduated and promoted to the state prisons. **Education Equates Equalization.**

In the mid 1990's Oprah show aired a program about the percentage of Americans with Black ancestry. Winfrey read to her audience the "One Drop Law" set by the supreme governing authority of the United States Government. The "One Drop Law" simply means that if a person has one drop of Negroid blood running through his veins, he is automatically Black. She also stated that 28 million Whites live in a racial closet, meaning that millions of people in this country have Black ancestry and in denial.

Observation sometimes uncovers answers. Look around, and you will see a lot of people with naturally curly hair—what does that tell you? The black dominant gene has the power to curl hair. If your hair is curly, you might be part of those Americans living in a racial closet.

Remember the question about "hair" entered as evidence in the OJ Simpson preliminary hearings. A witness was on the stand to substantiate the presence of hair found at the crime scene. The witness said that the Los Angeles laboratory still classifies hairs as Negroid, Caucasoid, or Mongoloid. Caucasoid hairs are fine and straight. Negroid hair is coarse and curly. Using the old standards of classification there are many people walking around with Negroid hairs growing from their heads. The original classification of hair doesn't fit the mold any more.

An article titled "Boxed In," appearing in *The New Republic,* reports that the United States Census Bureau has 15 classifications for Americans to check. A new box labeled "other" appeared in the 1990 survey. Ten million people checked that box. Because the Federal statistics cannot account for "other," the 10 million people who checked this box ended up proportionally divided among all categories.

There have been protests that this new multiracial box would dilute statistical strength of the Black Race. Labels are important to people especially the labels building self-worth for those people who want recognition as PART WHITE. Seventy-five to ninety (75-90%) of BLACK Americans are technically multiracial in this country without the mixed race box to check.

The geneticists study select blood groups, abnormal hemoglobin's, lactase deficiency, tooth size, body size, disease susceptibility, nutrition, structure of chromosomes, bone formation (ossification), genetic influences on fat, metabolism, congenital birth defects, inherited skeletal traits, biochemical analysis of the urine, and earwax--things that may already have been investigated.

The study of race mixture in the United States gives examples of people who socially identify as African Americans, for example, from Detroit, Oakland, or West Texas. Seventy-five percent (75%) of the Negroid Race in this country come from bloodlines considered mixed.

Oprah aired a show in the mid 1990's whose audience and panel guests were of mixed race. Some of the people on the panel want the US government to recognize their ethnic backgrounds that is BLACK as well as WHITE. They said they didn't feel BLACK because they knew they were half WHITE. What they don't realize is that they are BLACK with a White parent or people with African Ancestry. It sounds as if they are trying to boost their psychological well-being.

I think a person in the audience summed up exactly what is happening to children of mixed races when she stated that the WHITE MOTHERS of these children were probably in a STATE OF DENIAL for having Black children in the first place and have passed along their feelings to their children.

The White mothers could not accept having had Black children and have depressed the reality of the situation. In turn they have encouraged their children to be proud and voice their WHITE as well as their BLACK heritage. By being both White and Black the children **AREN'T REALLY BLACK**. It helps the White parent accept the situation in which they have found themselves.

White women use this denial as a defense mechanism to protect themselves from an unpleasant reality subjected to by her White family for marrying a Black man. People repress feelings and restructure thoughts when they say things like: "It doesn't matter what color you are because we are all members of the human race." "People are people first and foremost."

I remember what Halle Berry (actress) once said that made a lot of sense. She said that she was confused as a child because of her White mother and started asking questions about color. Her mother cleared up all of Halle's questions when she said, "You are a Black child with a White mother."

In the early Nineteenth Century some EuroAmerican scientist's known as "The American School," measured the size and shape of human skulls and claimed to have discovered an ascending chain from lower animals and primates. The closest to apes = Blacks. The apex of nature's achievements = Whites.

In the ante-bellum south there were tens of thousands of mulattos who were legally Black, but who were more than half White. Mulatto children learned to value their whiteness (Huggins, Kilson, Fox, 216). The mulattos valued their Whiteness and so would White mothers value their children's Whiteness after reading the foregoing scenario.

The main objective in this country is to keep America White although White may appear to have a permanent suntan of sorts. As one looks at the rest of the world with its majority black and brown faces, it must be scary for a nation of majority Whites to see that a change is taking place. That is why there is legislation on the books to consider children of mixed parentage NOT TO BE CONSIDERED BLACK (but of mixed-race or multiracial).

The White Race in America includes Mexican Americans, American Natives, and Arab Americans? Encyclopedias list them as part of the Caucasian Race. Will this work as a method to increase the WHITE NUMBERS and reduce the number of "people of color" in this country? WE ARE TURNING INTO A NATION OF BROWN PEOPLE!

The Census Bureau report stated that 30% of Native Americans checked themselves as White until the Indian box appeared on the census survey. The *Detroit News/Free Press* published an article titled "US Population Worries." It stated that if the US has to adopt a population policy with implications for immigration and family size. Births in this country amount to less than two-thirds of the annual population increase; whereas, Immigration--legal and illegal--accounts for more than a **million** new residents a year (Dickerson, B-1).

The Detroit News/Free Press ran an article titled, "Should We Close Our Borders?" (Eric Liu, *USA Weekend, p. 5*) The United States takes more than 1 million newcomers every year more than all other industrialized nations combined. Between 1980 and 1990, 9.5 million legal and illegal immigrants came here. In 1992, there were 76% legal vs. 24% illegal aliens who entered the country.

Persons made to feel helpless in life situations with unemployment/underemployment, lack of the BIG house, little or no education, etc. are more likely to act helpless in other situations if they attribute their failure to lasting, general factors. THE WHITE WOMAN comes along.

Emotions soar, and she becomes the means to an end. She becomes the stepping-stone to faith, hope, and charity. The White woman sees and feels mystique because of all of the media coverage and warning signals. The White community sends up subconscious fears and stereotypes in smoke signals. That is why there was such overwhelming coverage of the Thomas, Tyson, and Simpson cases.

Black man bashing has yielded the unconscious turned conscious feeling that White is right, and the White woman is thusly virtuous. **Self-hate Therapy ^*equals*^ A White-right woman!**

According to noted Psychologist, Albert Bandura (Stanford University 1977:1989), a person will develop an adequate personality after exposure to good models. An inadequate learning environment, on the other hand, will result in inadequate personality development. Bandura observed that the individual's behavior and the social learning environment continually influence one another. Perceptions of self-esteem (efficacy) develop from what others say about us, direct experiences of success and failure and other sources. The person classified a secondclass citizen certainly has lower self-esteem. Psychologically, he wants to be a first-class citizen. He must possess all of the things Mr. Supremacy possesses, including the White woman.

This cognition's continue to influence our behavior "FROM INSIDE OUT." Bandura concurs that we all learn our personal standards from observing the personal standards that other people model and from the standards that others use when rewarding or punishing us (Lahey, 338-9).

A unique feature of the humanistic approach is Abraham Maslow's description of self-actualization (1954). It is the need to develop one's potential fully, to lead a rich and meaningful life, and to become the best person one can become (Coon, 12).

Example: Purchasing clothes, jewelry, an automobile, cologne, membership in a health club, changing your hair to blonde and your eyes to blue/green and the choosing of a White woman may be influenced by images of a valued future self.

The development of a positive self-image depends greatly on information from the surrounding environment. It begins with a sorting of perceptions and feelings: my body, my nose, I want, I like, I am, and so on. Soon, it expands to include self-evaluation: I am a good person. I did something bad just now. I have a White woman, so I am on the same level and as good as you are—LOOK AT ME, and so forth. Black men receive an orgasmic valuing in a direct, gut-level response to life. Black men feel a positive regard from others if they can assimilate and are in possession of the same things the dominant culture has in his possession (Coon, 457-8).

In the 1950's, Rock 'n' Roll music made its debut. Rock 'n' Roll is an "off spring" of Jazz, Blues, and Black Gospel music—not the invention of Buddy Holly or the appointed accolade "King of Rock 'n' Roll" Elvis Presley. *Hound Dog* by Big Mamma Thornton released the title in 1953. Elvis Presley made it popular in 1956, but you would have thought he was the propagator.

In addition to Jazz, Blues, and Gospel music a great deal of today's American music derives its formation from the magnetic force of the syncopation in what came to be called "ragtime" or "Piano Rag Music" created by Scott Joplin (1868-1917). Some people think of "Ragtime" as something heard mainly in saloons, played (and most frequently improvised) by pianists wearing derby hats, smoking big cigars and going boom-te-di-boom with an um-pah-pah bass (Scott Joplin: King of Ragtime, Lewis Music Publishing Co. Carlstadt, NJ, 1922).

Blues and Jazz have always been an expression of the living conditions of the

Black Race in America. The White cultural society takes the "Black Experience" and turns it into recognition and monetary themselves.

The American Music Awards and Awards have created categories within the past 20 years for Best Rhythm & Blues Album and Singer, etc. The creation of R & B music categories stopped Black artists from infringing on what has been reserved for White artists. Black music tops listening and sales but slighted when passing out awards.

Remember the first *Rocky* (1976) movie starring Sylvester Stallone and the II and the III and the IV and the V? *Rocky's* picture (Sylvester Stallone) appeared on the front cover of *Time* magazine. Since the US did not have a Caucasian heavyweight champion to celebrate, they had to create their own mythical champion. Isn't it enough to blow the mind?
rewards for

the Grammy

CONCLUSION

Americans receive daily doses from the "old guard" i.e. American "stink tank." It has caused a laughable level of conscious awareness. The subconscious brain character is play'in y'all. The Psyche Race War has made American Whites comatose while Blacks continually act out created "Dumb Nigga Roles." The current "Mother" of all wars surpasses WWI, WWII, Korea, Vietnam and the Iraq War combined. The evidence is part of our day-to-day existence. The Government and its "National Security" invests heavily in police operations, prisons, weaponry and surveillance systems to maintain an established order in Black/Brown neighborhoods and "lock em up!"

The Official "War on Niggas" is not apparent to most citizens. In the US Blacks live a day-to-day "blackness awareness." While walking down the street, going to work or attending school, "Black" is what characterizes our being. Envision the reality. Blacks do not exist in the White conscious world. In fact, Blacks are as invisible as the character in Ralph Ellison's book Invisible Man. A created eagerness for Black people to jump on the "whitewashed bandwagon" and noticed by Whites is expected—you'll been trained. We profess with boastfulness, "Oh!" "I'm part White," "I'm part Indian," or "I'm multiracial.

Being part White or part Indian gives the average Black person a mimicking superiority self-image. "It is all about recognizing our White mothers and grandmothers they say!" Over 80% of all Black Americans have an admixture with Native American blood and/or White blood scientifically defined as African Ancestry. Blacks in America are already multiracial without having a new racial category on the books--thanks to the slave master and escaping back-in-the-day. With that commonality— what's the express Caucasian joy? Think about it. White people still recognize you as Black. They won't realize your color distinction unless they are White mothers with Black children.

The White culture has performed a fundamental function to augment "laws of the land." The American Legal System assists Whites to make them feel they are permanent, safe and never-ending. jump in UNISON on the back of establishing identities with White Race principles because Caucasian ideologies promise to connect—a significance that will never perish.

Blacks identify with Caucasians and adopt their culturally sanctioned viewpoints. Survival means investing in the American System and ascribing absolute and permanent truth in the White man's secure state. Inflation of all brings a sense of secure righteousness declaring that whatever is "White right!" We protect ourselves against the exposure of truth insisting that all other ideas or theories are false. In the end we attack and degrade our ancestors, our parents, ourselves and other Black Race members. We DENY absolute-truth systems that designate a Black man origin on Earth and the 8% myth of White man majority.

The guns are turned inward—"shoot em up,"— while outward our innards spew foul feces for future generations. The US Security System is working toward a speedy Black massacre. Drive-bys, crack pipes and illiteracy have been able to fulfill the holocaust measures in a relatively short period of time. It takes much more work to kill the stamina of the human psyche with selfhatred.

It causes Blacks to the wagon while

As the Black skin pigment disappears under the radiation of the cruel invisible hate-imp, it molds the Black Race into statues standing tall to model the "Old Guard"—Confederacy Flag fly on—American "stink tank." The flags lowered, but the embedded mindset typically shines in the US populace.

Revisionist History is the tone of the day. The Host Race IS NOT the White Race as we have been led to believe. The respective White recessive population is about to lose its biological identity. The Caucasian Race is at a MINUS 0% replacement level. While the US and European history books theorize and toil in the differences between Caucasian populations who live in Eastern and Western Europe, Northern Africa, Australia and the United States, it all "GOES BACK TO BLACK."

The Black man links his secret inner self, his authentic talent, his deepest feelings of uniqueness ... to the very ground of White man creation. Out of the ruins of the broken cultural self, there remains the mystery of the private, invisible, inner self, which yearns for ultimate significance. The Black Host Race attains significance by affirming connection with the ONCE UPON-A-TIME mystery of Black creation and White Albinism. White global power exists only through media reports in EuroAmerica and parts of Australia. Just as Greece fell and Greek Mythology found its place in world literature, the mythological White Race will find itself in historical literature as the recessive gene........ THAT ONCE WAS!

White Woman Warrantee: The 1990's Era witnessed a "panic attack" on the "big Black penis." The American media whored African-American men to validate an all-around
derogations. In both
proof of Black men sexual

the Clarence Thomas Senate Hearings of 1991 and the arrest and trial of OJ Simpson in 1994-5, television networks worked hard to present evidence, to project views, and to taunt and educate White women in this country of the deviant Black male.

Clarence was at the top of the apex with education and position and christened—all time "sexual harasser." Michael Jackson was once the ultimate entertainer turned child molester and pedophile-- endowed "dinky" or "dinkily" of the crew. Hail--OJ Simpson: "White woman abuser and murderer." Mike Tyson was the "illiterate rapist" while Dennis Rodman was dubbed "clown prince." Tiger Negrito Woods escaped the accusers and married a white woman--Why wouldn't he? He's not Black any more. He is a "Cablinasian"--even though his parents are Black in color--even his Negrito mother. In fact, his mother probably has more Negro DNA than his Black father. America learned that Black men were all-around large penis dicks regardless of their positions in American life. The proof presented to America resulted in White women running to accept black more vs. white less. The large penis CAUTIONS reversed the original warning and caused their women to want what they were not getting. They suffer from "White Man Mania" as their women glide to the Black side.

You must read carefully between the lines and translate the code words. For centuries Whites have used benign code words on the surface to promote a White superiority strategy. Since Blacks are survivors of a dichotomy world, it should be easy to train oneself to read between the lines of benign codes used as psychological brain warfare maneuvers.

Mental White Man Mania—The US is reaping the impairment of the "angry White male" who has been given the term "sudden murderer" by psychologists. The White male reeks of fanatical views that he is the "mostess" credible and "bestess" authentic that can persuade the enemy to trust him—although he remains the enemy. He is the "Super Power Global Cop." When there were mass shootings near the end of the Millennium at the Federal Building in Oklahoma City, Columbine High School in Littleton, Colorado, and schools in Paducah, Kentucky and Atlanta, Georgia the shootings became media abnormalities. National news programs tore apart and dissected the irregular/random White man behavior. The television news cameras rent space in the Black community. Homicides in the Black community are routine and common occurrences.

When jumping on the Whiteness bandwagon to become "part White" or "multiracial," think twice before pulling up on the joystick and losing your wheels. As you face your Black and Brown Race aggressors, you will only amount to 8% of the global population. Translate the code words. For centuries Whites have used benign code words on the surface. Since Blacks are survivors of a dichotomy words and have always been under the radiation of an invisible imp titled "E-Lite," the long-time running big screen spectacle Oreo Cookie reversed out Vanilla Wafer is an academy winning full-length feature publicized "twenty-four seven." Performing Black men turn slowly inside out symbolizing a pigment disappears, and continuing stupidly to live in the big screen exhibition shining their E-lites.

Observable behavior and the process of learning go hand-in-hand as we watch what naturally occurs. The ability has been lost to distinguish between imagination and what is real. We have stepped out of our "psychological Black selves" and no longer see Black— even though our commonality is color. We have evolved into mainstream White America accepting the "n-a-t-u-ra-l order" disproportionate allotment for everything in life to which Whites are continually given the first choice.

Slavery in the Name of Jesus—White superiority was born within Christianity. The Roman Church of 1455 cream filled albino. Their

they become transparent, authorized infidel (atheist) people to servitude in 1457. The Council of Cardinals met in Holland and sanctioned as a righteous and progressive idea, the enslavement of Black Africans for the purpose of their conversion to Christianity and for acquisition in the labor market as chattel property. final outcome helplessness. Some slaves longed to be a replication of the "chosen ones"—Master White Race. They loved their masters because they bask in the "reflected White Glory"—which in turn enhanced both Black and White psychological delusional power (Glory to His Name). This attachment was necessary for the formation of present day psycho-political symbiosis.

The new Millennium brings with it a new world order. The global world is no longer homogenously White. A "changing of the guards" occurred while America was busy painting its inhabitants White. You probably didn't notice because people with Negroid stock were busy changing their racial classification. While Blacks were proving to White America that they were—at least—part white—a series of events at the end of the Millennium spelled out White global annihilation.

Slaves were incapable to foresee the and ingested the inborn learned

Epilogue

Intentions were not to categorize any group of people. Correcting false historical records was the aim because the color of history was changed. Examples of physical features and examples of dress/fashion emphasize certain points and give readers an urgent **WAKE - UP CALL!**

If a great flood like that of Noah's time were upon the US, and there was room for one more person on the boat, a Black person dressed in a suit and tie would be left to drown, as the White person with no teeth, smell'in to high heaven, and shabby clothes is lifted to safety. We have proof of that. Remember New Orleans and Hurricane Katrina?

The theory or belief or conception that some races have brown skin because the sun has darkened the skin has a foundation built on sand. The White recessive gene is disappearing quickly even though fertility drugs are available to White women who have problems conceiving. Right now the Europe-America is working with quotas based on racial identity. Pretty soon identity will not exist because the majority of the global world is of varying degrees of mixed African descent. The browns are being given the "honor badge" Caucasian.

The attraction of the White woman to the Black man is like an epidemic that is spreading to fast to stop. To stop its progress is impossible because it is a "silent racial revolt/evolution."

The research for this book draws a very clear picture of what has happened in the past five to ten thousand years. The Neanderthal and Cro-Magnon Man were forerunners to modern man, and scientists have linked the original man to the Bushmen-Hottentots of South Africa.

This whole book substantiates the Negroid substrata in all parts of the world. An African fossil was found in Düsseldorf (Europe) dating back to the Stone Age. There is also linguistics linking African languages to other parts of the world. There are books written about vanished Negro civilizations. White people would rather believe mankind evolved from apes than from a Black man in Africa who then migrated to all parts of the world.

Excavations in Mexico (Olmec Colossal Heads) and so called (mysterious hieroglyphics) found in Northern New York, have proven Blacks were here before Leif Erickson and Christopher Columbus. Every person **evolved from Black.** The color spectrum alone proves that.

Pictures of the Neanderthal and Cro-Magnon man Encyclopedias and research books look like **White** men who are half man and half animal. The pictures drawn and painted by Whites depict their own life imitations. These examples are like the "White Jesus" pictures hanging in churches. Christ has been drawn and painted according to the artist's image of how he looks at the world.

Both Black and White people learn from repeated association. White domination in this country has caused an elicited response resulting in a permanent change of thinking consciously and subconsciously. This domination has linked us to the sight, conscience, and belief that validity only prevails in White cultural surroundings.

The Black Cro-Magnon man gave-way or evolved to the present form of modern mankind. If Blacks were more knowledgeable of their history and culture, there would be no such thing as a Value Whiteness Stigma. Blacks would not want to assimilate into the White culture.

Blacks would not want to pass for White or placed on the **multiracial** enclosure bin. There is **POWER** in numbers. African-American history and pride are probably the furthest things from one's mind when the crack pipe or waiting for the postal carrier to bring the Welfare check are top priority on one's agenda. Somehow the White Press—Media Elites have tried to twist and turn American history into a subliminal mockery. The preceding statements made discount the march and to assure White America that they are still in charge and have the upper hand. The Special Issues published by the White Press are in print, on CD ROM, and on microfiche.

The media elites will continue to use its **Hypnotic Susceptibility Scale** to convince the general public that Blacks are the poster children for crime and ignorance as long as the tactics work. When a rat is cornered, it comes out wild and in the attack mode. Controversy causes a person to weigh the issues. The truth is before you-**wake up!**

The latest scientific theory professed by many anthropologists that the "Races of Mankind" **NO LONGER EXIST substantiates a theory of human evolvement.** matter. ALL classified as White.

As the White Aryans shrink into non-existence, scientists and anthropologists will scurry to put into place a new Brown/White Race that no longer recognizes color. We will be classified as "White Negroes." One day we will all wake up and be **White.**

In 100 years, maybe none of this will people evolvement will be Brown and

BIBLIOGRAPHY

Chapter I

Bowman, Elizabeth Atkins. "Smith's Fake Black 'Suspect' Based on a Bitter History of Racial Stereotypes" Detroit News/Free Press. 6 November 1994.

Boyd, Robert S. "Coloring Intelligence," Detroit Free Press, 23 October 1994.
Case, Ellis. "Everybody's Talking at Me" Newsweek, 14 May 1994.
Huggins, Nathan I., Kilson, Martin, and Fox, Daniel M. Key Issues of the Afro-American Experience, San Diego: Harcourt Brace Jovanovich Publishers, 1971.
Katz, William Loren. The Black West, Seattle, WA: Open Hand Publishing, Co., 1987.
Logan, Rayford W., & Cohen, Irving S. The American Negro, Boston: Houghton Mifflin Co., 1967.
Love, Tru. Ebony, "What I learned as a White Girl in a Black School," September 1993.
National Directory of Children, Youth & Family Services, Marion L. Peterson Publisher, 1993-94.
Ploski, Harry A., & Williams, James. The Negro Almanac: A Reference Work on the Afro-American - 4th Ed. New York: John Wiley & Sons, 1983.
Samuelson, Robert J. "Sowing More Cynicism," Newsweek 24 October, 1994.
Sklar, Holly. "The Upper Class and Mothers N the Hood, Boston: Z Magazine, March 1993.
Tharp, Mike & Streisand, Betsy. "Tabloid TV's Blood Lust" U. S. News World Report, 25 July 1994.
Time, 20 March 1995.
United Stated Government - Internal Revenue Service, Federal Tax Guide Reports for Tax Year 1994, Sections #5178 - 80.
Walvin, James Slavery and the Slave Trade, Jackson: University Press of Mississippi, 1983.
Weinstein, Amy. ed. Public Welfare Directory, Washington D. C.: American Public Welfare Association, 1989.

Chapter II

Dillion, Richard H. North American Indian Wars, New York: Gallery Books, 1983.
Hoffman, Kathy Barks & Basheda, Valarie, "Statistics link race to type of crime, who's arrested," Detroit News & Free Press, 22 January 1995.
Marriott, Michael. "I Do?", Essence, November 1993.
Ruiz, Ramon Eduardo. Cuba: The Making of A Revolution, New York: W. W. Norton & Company, 1968.

Sklar, Holly. "The Upper Class and Mothers N the Hood, Boston: Z Magazine, March 1993.

Chapter III

Adler, Jerry. "Murder: A week in the Death of America," Newsweek, 15 August 1994.
Alexander, Alison & Hanson, Jarice. Taking Sides, Guilford, CN: The Dushkin Publishing Group, Inc., 1993.
Brinken, Wendy. James Marion Sims: Father Butcher. www.seedshow.com/jmsims.htm.
City of Southfield Zoning Ordiances, Chapter 45, Southfield, MI: City of Southfield, October 1988.
Gibbs, Nancy. "The Vicious Cycle," Time, 20 June 1994.

Huggins, Nathan I., Kilson, Martin, and Fox, Daniel M. Key Issues of the Afro-American Experience, San Diego: Harcourt Brace Jovanovich Publishers, 1971.

Leland, John. "Just Say Maybe," Newsweek, 1 November 1993. McGarrell, Edmund F. Crime and Delinquincy, Newbury Park: SAGE

Periodicals Press, Inc., Vol. 39-#1 January 1993.
Quarles, Benjamin. The Negro in the Making of America, New York:
Macmillan Publishing Co, 1987.
Savage, Ashid A. *The Black Eye*, Detroit: April 1995.
Welsing, Dr. Frances Cress. The Isis Papers, Chicago: Third World Press, 1991.

Chapter IV

Boyd, William & Asimov, Isaac. Races and People, New York: Abelard-Schuman Publishers, 1955.
Dickerson, Brian. "Upfront," Detroit Free Press Magazine, 16, October 1994.
Friend, Tad. "Garbage in, Garbage Out: The White Trashing of America," Detroit Free Press Magazine, 16, October 1994.

Gould, Stephen Jay. "The Geometer of Race," Discover, November 1994.
Jet, "Black-White Marriages," 8, March 1993.
MacDonald J., Fred. Blacks and White TV, Chicago: Nelson Hall Publishers, 1992.
Morganthau, Tom. "I Q: Is it Destiny?" Newsweek, 24 October, 1994.
Shreeve, James. "Terms of Estrangement," Discover, November 1994.
Welsing, Dr. Frances Cress. The Isis Papers, Chicago: Third World Press, 1991.

Chapter V

Alexander, Alison & Hanson, Jarice. Taking Sides, Guilford, CN: The Dushkin Publishing Group, Inc., 1993.
Bates, Karen Gregsby. "Why are we Still Color Struck?" Essence, September 1994.
Frazier, Lisa & Warner, Coleman. "Together Apart: The Myth of Race--Early Lessons Last a Lifetime." *Times-Picayune.* 12 September, 1993.
Gannon, James P. "Journalists," Detroit News Free Press, 24 July 1994.
Lahey, Benjamin B. Psychology: An Introduction, Miami: William C. Brown Publishers, 1992.

Chapter VI

Boyd, William & Asimov, Isaac. Races and People, New York: Abelard-Schuman Publishers, 1955.
Detroit News, "Scientists Push Classifications Not Based on Race," 16 April, 1995.
Diop, Cheikh Anta. The African Origin of Civilization: Myth or Reality, Chicago: Lawrence Hill

Books, 1967.
Encyclopedia Britannia, Vol. 15, Chicago: Encyclopedia Britannia, Inc., 1979.
Gould, Stephen Jay. "The Geometer of Race," Discover, November 1994.
Newsweek October 24, 1994 "IQ: Is it Destiny"
Shreeve, James. "Erectus Rising" Discover, September 1994.

Chapter VII

Bennett, Lerone Jr. Before the Mayflower: A History of Black America, Chicago: Johnson Publishing Co., Inc. 1982.

Diop, Cheikh Anta. The African Origin of Civilization: Myth or Reality, Chicago: Lawrence Hill Books, 1967.
Hanes, Bailey C. (Colonel). Bill Pickett: Bulldoger, Norman: University of Oklahoma Press, 1979.
Hilton, David Edmond. Lieutenant Henry O. Flipper, Odessa, Texas, 1989.
Jantzen, Steven L., Neill, Kenneth, Krieger, Larry S., World History: Perspectives on the Past, Lexington, MA: D. C. Heath and Company, 1988.
Katz, William Loren. The Black West, Seattle, WA: Open Hand Publishing, Co., 1987.
Korngold, Ralph. Citizen Toussaint, New York: Hill & Wang, 1965.
Leckie, William H. The Buffalo Soldiers, The University of Oklahoma Press, 1967.
Logan, Rayford W., & Cohen, Irving S. The American Negro, Boston: Houghton Mifflin Co., 1967.
Pohl, Frederick Julius. Atlantic Crossings Before Columbus, New York: W. W. Norton & Co., Inc., 1961.
Quarles, Benjamin. The Negro in the Making of America, New York: Macmillan Publishing Co, 1987.
Sertima, Ivan Van. They Came Before Columbus: The African Presence in Ancient America, New York: Random House 1976.
Shreeve, James. "Erectus Rising" Discover, September 1994.

Chapter VIII

African Heritage Study Bible, Ed. Rev. Cain Hope Felder, Ph.D, Iowa Falls, IA: World Bible Publishers, Inc. 1993.
Boyer-Larkin, Robin, "Black Origins," The Michigan Chronicle, 8-14 March 1995.
Diop, Cheikh Anta. The African Origin of Civilization: Myth or Reality, Chicago: Lawrence Hill Books, 1967.
Encyclopedia Britannia, Vol. 15, Chicago: Encyclopedia Britannia, Inc., 1979.
Higgins, Godfrey, (Esq.).Anacalypsis: An Attempt to Draw Aside the Veil of the Saitic Isis; or an Inquiry into the Origin of Languages, Nations, and Religions,
Huggins, Nathan Irvin. Black Odyssey, New York: Vintage Books, 1989.
London: Life Science Vol. I,1836.
Lemonick, Michael D. "How Man Began," Time, 14 March 1994.

Plano, Jack C. & Greenberg, Milton. The American Political Dictionary, (6th ed.) New York: Holt, Rinehart, & Winston, 1982.

Prehistoric Man, Vol. I, London: 1876.
Rogers, J. A., Sex and Race, St. Petersburg, FL: H. M. Rogers, Vol. I,

1967.
Sertima, Ivan Van. They Came Before Columbus: The African Presence in Ancient America, New York: Random House 1976.

Chapter IX

The African American Encyclopedia, Vol. 6. New York: 1993. Bogert, Carroll. "Good News on Drugs from the Inner City,"

Newsweek, 14 February 1994.
Chethik, Neil, "Accusations Against Black Men Mask Real Trouble,"
The Detroit News/Free Press, 9 October 1994.
Gladwell, Malcolm ."It's Entirely Possibly, But Not Very Likely,"
Washington Post National Weekly Edition. 13-19 April.
Washington D. C., 1992.
Neesday, Laurie Garrett. "Scientists Trying to Trace Evolutionary
Path of HIV," Albuquerque Journal 2 January 1994. Steinbrook, Robert "Ancestors of AIDS," 12,
April, Wichita, Kansas:
Wichita Eagle, 1992.

Chapter X

Coon, Dennis. Introduction to Psychology: Exploration and Application, St. Paul: West Publishing Co.,
1989.
Dickerson, Marla. "U. S. Population Worries Growing," The Detroit News/Free Press, 28 August 1994.
Encyclopedia Americana, Chicago: Encyclopedia Americana, Inc. Vol. II, 1990.
George, Nelson. "Deglamorizing Street Style," Essence, November, 1993.
Huggins, Nathan I. Kilson, Martin, and Fox, Daniel M. Key Issues of the Afro-American Experience,
San Diego: Harcourt Brace Jovanovich Publishers, 1971.
Jones, Charisse. "Rap's Bad Rep," Los Angeles Times, 2 May 1993.
Kael, Pauline. 5001 Nights at the Movies, New York: Henry Holt Company, 1991.
Lahey, Benjamin B. Psychology: An Introduction, Miami: William C. Brown Publishers, 1992.

Lewis, Gregory. "Taking the Rap: Where to Draw the Line," San Francisco Examiner & Chronicle, 12
January 1992.
Lie, Eric *Detroit News/Free Press*, "Should We Close Our Borders?" 25 September 1994.
Rosin, Hanna. "Boxed In," The New Republic, 3 January 1994.

Chapter XI

Berger, Arthur Asa, Media Analysis Techniques, Newbury Park, CA: Sage Publications, Inc.1991.
Eshleman, J. Ross, Cashion, Barbara G., Basirico, Lawrence A. Sociology: An Introduction. New
York: Harper Collins, College Publishers, Inc. 1993.
Newsweek, "What Color is Black?" 13 February 1995.
Ploski, Harry A., & Williams, James. The Negro Almanac: A Reference Work on the Afro-American -
4th Ed. New York: John Wiley & Sons, 1983.
Walvin, James Slavery and the Slave Trade, Jackson: University Press of Mississippi, 1983.